This little book
and old—to kn
a beautiful plan

20s, and my only regret is that I didn't come to know it sooner. I pray this book will help many young people find joy, delight, and contentment in knowing God.

Brian Brodersen, pastor emeritus of Calvary Chapel, Costa Mesa, California

Jeremy has written the definitive book for redeeming young-adult life and charting a course for lasting influence. You don't have to squander your 20s pursuing a life of meaningless parties, mindlessly playing or making plans that are shallow and self-centered. By prioritizing these seven godly pursuits, you will leave a mark for Christ and his kingdom on your generation that will reach into eternity. Make It Your Ambition is a blueprint for succeeding at what matters most.

Chris Brooks, senior pastor of Woodside Bible Church; host of *Equipped*, Moody Radio

Make It Your Ambition covers key discipleship topics for young adults with biblical clarity and spiritual earnestness in a relatable style. In a society that prizes achievement over character, this book refreshingly commends the ambitious pursuit of knowing and reflecting Jesus Christ in all we do. May God grant this goal abundantly to all who read it.

Jonathan K. Dodson, theologian-in-residence at Citizens Church, author of numerous books including *The Unbelievable Gospel* and *Our Good Crisis*, and founder of Gospel-Centered Discipleship

The word "ambition" is usually applied to certain pursuits: Get straight A's. Climb the corporate ladder. Blow up on YouTube.

But this book flips ambition on its head, encouraging you to become like Christ and serve God's kingdom. Jeremy unpacks the Bible's teachings on identity and calling in a way that will not only inspire you to live for God but actually show you how to do it. There are a thousand messages out there clamoring for your attention. This book contains true wisdom. Make it your ambition to follow Jesus and you will live a life that truly matters.

> **Drew Dyck**, author of *Your Future Self Will Thank You* and *Just Show Up*

I wrestled for several years over God's call on my life. As I prayed, I also asked older Christians for advice and book recommendations. I would've greatly benefited from Jeremy Writebol's *Make It Your Ambition*. I'm so glad a new generation will have this resource to help them develop godly ambition to serve the church and fulfill the Great Commission.

> **Collin Hansen**, vice president for content at The Gospel Coalition and host of the *Gospelbound* podcast

Christian young adults today strive to pursue Christ under the relentless downpour of our information age. Jeremy Writebol does a masterful job providing them with practical wisdom. Chock full of creative perspectives and grounded in Christ-centered principles, *Make It Your Ambition* will inspire you and help you refocus your life.

> **Ronnie Martin**, director of leader care and renewal for Harbor Network; pastor-in-residence at Redeemer Community Church in Bloomington, Indiana; author of numerous books; and cohost of the *Heart of Pastoring* podcast

Moving to the mission field in my early 20s was the beginning of the best years of my life. Now, over 25 years into vocational ministry, I can say that I have no regrets and would do it all again.

And again. I'd love nothing more than to see a wave of young people pursue the same. In *Make It Your Ambition*, Jeremy Writebol conveys why it's a good, worthy, truly wonderful way to spend one's life. He demystifies the journey into ministry and offers the needed encouragement of an older sibling or mentor in the faith. Whether you're young and are discerning God's call on your life or older and wondering about making a change, this book holds the wisdom you need, and it will keep you tethered to God's grace, which will carry you through whatever you do.

Jen Oshman, speaker, missionary, women's ministry leader, and author of multiple books including *Cultural Counterfeits* and *Welcome*

Every young adult has an innate desire to find purpose and meaning in the work they do and the life they live. Jeremy Writebol's new book *Make It Your Ambition* is filled with biblically rich wisdom and practical application for young adults seeking to know their purpose and find their calling. It's full of conviction for the apathetic, hope for the disappointed, and new perspective for the successful.

Emma Kruger Tang, recent college graduate, University of North Carolina, Chapel Hill

Make It Your Ambition

7 Godly Pursuits for the Next Generation

Jeremy Writebol

TGC

Make It Your Ambition: Seven Godly Pursuits for the Next Generation

Published by The Gospel Coalition

P.O. Box 1637
Columbia, Missouri 65205

Cover Design: Laura Schembre
Typesetting: Ryan Leichty

ISBN:
978-1-956593-15-0 (paperback)
978-1-956593-16-7 (ebook)
978-1-956593-17-4 (kindle)

Printed in the United States of America

For Allison and Ethan
Leave it all on the field, for the glory of God!

Contents

Foreword

Don't waste your 20s. This is what I tell young people finishing high school and getting ready to head off to college or a trade school, or 20-somethings starting a new job, or young couples talking about marriage, or young men and women discerning a call into some kind of ministry in the church.

At some point in the past 50 years, many in our society began to see the 20s as the season of life where you could just "figure things out" and have as much fun as possible doing so. This mentality pushed back the average age for getting married. The housing crisis and other economic developments solidified a trend toward young adults moving back in with their parents. Surveys revealed a steep decline in churchgoing among young people raised in the Christian faith. The term "extended adolescence" captures this lengthier transition from the teenage years into (maybe) college and beyond.

On the surface and by themselves, none of these developments is bad (aside from the church dropout phenomenon). No one expects you to know exactly what your life will look like in 10 to 15 years, so yes, you'll be spending time "figuring things out" and enjoying friends and family as you do so. It may be a while before you find a spouse and get married (if the Lord has plans for you to marry at all). It may be the best and wisest stewardship of money to arrange to live at home at some point in the next few years. And if you're reading this book, you probably intend to stay in your home church or find another church wherever college life or your career takes you, thus bucking the trend of "taking off" from church during your 20s.

Whatever the future holds, I'll tell you what I tell others: don't waste your 20s. This decade can be the launching pad for the rest of your life. You'll encounter opportunities to have an eternal influence, leaving ripple effects for generations to come. What's more, you're on mission now. You don't need a title, a ministry position, or a college degree before you live on mission. Jesus's commissioning is all you need to love God, love people, and witness to the truth of the gospel.

Your generation is sometimes described as one marked by widespread spiritual apathy. Jeremy Writebol wants to ignite your imagination so you see what a life marked by robust, gospel-fueled, Spirit-filled activity can look like. For those who struggle against apathy, he wants to inspire you with a holy ambition. For those who hold big career ambitions, he wants to ensure your aspirations are big enough—that they reach beyond the successes and goals of this life and reach toward everything God has for you.

This little book is like hopping from mountaintop to mountaintop, scaling the heights of what your life could be in your 20s and beyond. It starts with the orienting principle of the kingdom of God, what Jesus told us to seek first. Jeremy then presents seven worthy pursuits, the first as a fountain from which the rest flow—a life marked by what we were made for, to know and love God.

- He presents the beauty of the gospel and then brings us face-to-face with Jesus, the One we receive as a gift before we follow him as our example.
- He urges us to take stock of the gifts and talents the Lord has given us so they might be deployed for kingdom purposes.
- He upends the self-centered, self-actualizing mindset we naturally bring to our career by showing us Jesus's call to service through our work.
- He beckons us toward the adventure of evangelism, of sharing and showing Jesus's love in words backed up by deeds.
- And he calls us to persevere when life is tough and the inevitable seasons of suffering descend on us.

Six of the seven pursuits apply to everyone reading this book. The final one will not. But I suspect the seventh ambition Jeremy describes may be the very tool God uses to bring some into vocational ministry in the church, in charities, or in other Christian ministries.

As you turn the page from one chapter to the next in the story of your life, I hope you'll carefully consider the seven ambitions Jeremy puts before you here. These pursuits will affect how your story unfolds.

This isn't a book to read and set aside; it's a guide to live by. As you walk through these pages, don't just admire the wisdom offered—apply it. The seven godly pursuits Jeremy outlines here aren't just ideals to strive toward; they're divine invitations into a life of meaning and purpose. Whether you feel confident in your calling or uncertain about the future, this book will point you to a bigger, bolder vision than what the world offers. A life anchored in God's kingdom isn't marked by drifting but by deliberate pursuit. Wrestle with these ambitions. Pray over them. Let them shape your outlook, not just for your 20s but for your entire life.

Trevin Wax
Vice President of Research and Resource Development
North American Mission Board

Introduction

What Will You Do for the Kingdom of God?

Do you remember thinking about your future when you were younger? All kinds of opportunities and dreams lay ahead. Everything dangled in front of you. You were invited to dream big about being an adult—about the kind of life you'd have and the work you'd do. Parents, teachers, and friends would ask, "What do you want to do when you grow up?" and you'd speculate about being a doctor, teacher, or athlete. You may have dreamed about being a hero: a firefighter, astronaut, nurse, or police officer. Maybe you were extra brave and ambitious and even ventured to dream about being president of the United States.

Years have passed, and here you are—a little closer to that pivotal point in time. The realities of adulthood are on your doorstep. You might be getting ready to go off to college. Or, perhaps, you're about to finish your undergraduate degree. Perhaps it's a good time to pause and reconsider that question you were asked as a child: "*What do you want to do when you grow up?*" Some of you will have let go of dreams; others still hold to the same aspirations. You may be on the same career trajectory you imagined when you first started thinking about the future, or you may now be on a different one.

I vividly remember being asked this question when I was in middle school. That conversation altered the course of my life. I was chatting with Ms. Little because I was interested in her daughter, and she wanted to know what kind of guy might be hanging around in the future. I was confident and glad she asked about my ambitions, because I was a responsible eighth grader who had figured a few things out (or so I thought).

As much as I loved sports (baseball in particular), I knew I wasn't gifted with the skills and coordination of a professional athlete—though I could sign an autograph like one. Playing baseball was out. But working in the realm of professional baseball was still possible. In fact, if there was anything I could do, it was talk. As a child, I'd listen to the St. Louis Cardinals and Minnesota Twins games on the radio. Broadcasters like Jack Buck, Mike Shannon, Herb Carneal, and John Gordon painted unfolding pictures of the game in my imagination as I listened and hoped for a hometown victory. I'd sit and play R.B.I. Baseball on my Nintendo Game Boy while broadcasting the play-by-play and analytical color commentary to anyone who'd listen.

So when Ms. Little asked about my goals, I told her outright, "I am going to be a professional baseball broadcaster." It was a firm answer, and I was satisfied with it. I don't know if that wasn't satisfying to her or if she was thinking about the bigger picture. She asked a follow-up question that disrupted all my best-laid plans and set my life on a completely different course: "What will you do for the kingdom of God?"

As quick as I was with my first answer, I was stymied by her second question. I wasn't thinking in this category. I fumbled out some answer along the lines of "Well, uhh, I, uhhh, I'll be a *Christian* broadcaster!" Surely that'd be enough to get her to trust me and let me hang out with her daughter. Granted, it wasn't a terrible answer. But it wasn't well thought out either. She had, in a single question, introduced a concept I hadn't yet considered—the idea of living for a greater purpose. This was a gentle challenge not to think exclusively about what *I* wanted to do with my life. It was an invitation to consider what *God* wanted me to do.

That moment was the beginning of a journey toward clarity and focus in the more mature calling of my adulthood. Those questions started me along the path that eventually culminated in my vocation as a pastor. I've now been in full-time vocational ministry for more than 20 years, and I have no intention of changing careers or doing anything else. This is what I'm supposed to do, what I was called to do, and what I love to do. But I didn't know that when I was 14. I didn't know it when I was 18. I didn't have complete clarity about this call until my mid-20s. But the trajectory was there. Ms. Little's two questions were the spark that urged me to consider and ultimately commit to full-time Christian ministry.

What about you? I imagine a pastor or a leader in your campus ministry handed you this book and encouraged you to read it. Perhaps one of your parents or a friend has been talking with you about your future and suggested you spend a little time here with me to think about your future. Excellent!

I want to be a friend, and I do want to talk with you about your future. Specifically, I'm curious about the two questions Ms. Little asked me. Let me ask you the first one: *What do you want to do when you grow up?* What are your career aspirations and dreams? Are you thinking of engineering, education, or a medical profession? How about politics or civil service? Perhaps you've got computer programming or design on your mind. Are you dreaming about being a lawyer, stockbroker, realtor, or dentist? Maybe you'd like to be a writer or a singer? There are multitudes of career opportunities, and I'm sure that by this point in your life, you've narrowed it down. What ideas or options do you have in front of you?

It's OK if you're like middle-school me and fire off a quick answer. I get it; you're eager to move forward with your life and get after the job of your dreams. As you think about your goals and plans, let me go one step further with the next question Ms. Little asked me: *What will you do for the kingdom of God?*

You may be stumped. Or perhaps you aren't and you're ready to tell me more. If so, that's great. But if you don't have any of it figured out yet, I want to help. Growing up and moving into your adult years won't be easy. Neither will figuring out the answers to big questions: *What is my purpose in life? What vocation (or vocations) should I pursue?*

That's where this book comes in. I want to engage you in thinking about your future life and career. I want to put an invitation into your heart that could change the trajectory of your life. I hope to get you to consider something you may have never remotely considered before.

Main Goal

Before I get to that invitation, however, I want to help set you up well for adulthood as a follower of Jesus Christ. If your future seems wide open and the possibilities overwhelming, I want to help you establish a trajectory for a life lived well for God's glory—*no matter what career path you follow*.

When I read the Bible and think about what we should and could be doing in life, I see a handful of pursuits for Christians to consider. For instance, Paul said in Romans 15:20 that he made it his ambition "to preach the gospel, not where Christ has already been named, lest [he build] on someone else's foundation." In 1 Thessalonians 4:11, he encourages us to "aspire to live quietly, and to mind [our] own affairs, and to work with [our] hands." These are important goals. But maybe we should start even wider—with an overarching aim that blankets all of life.

Colossians 3:17 encourages us, "Whatever you do, in word or deed, do everything in the name of the Lord Jesus, giving thanks to God the Father through him." This challenge sweeps down into every nook and cranny of our lives—into all our speech and actions, whatever we say or do. Paul's invitation to look to Christ with gratitude gives us solid ground from which we can navigate all our future pursuits. Every moment of our lives now and every dream we have for tomorrow are to be lived for the sole purpose of honoring King Jesus.

Paul here asks you about your life ambitions. What will you do with your life? Who will you ultimately do it for? What will you do for God's kingdom?

As I mentioned, Paul wrote about certain noble ambitions and worthy pursuits throughout his letters. Some of these are for every Christian to pursue and live out. Others are specific to Paul and his life, but they may still give shape to our own. I believe those ambitions can be organized into seven pursuits that give focus, clarity, and insight into what you may do with your life. They're a way you can take hold of Colossians 3:17 and make it your ambition to "do everything in the name of the Lord Jesus."

Steps Toward Clarity

As you think about what you'll do for your career and how that will serve God's kingdom, I want to show you a series of biblical pursuits you can undertake—pursuits that will show you how your career and your service for God's kingdom aren't separate tracks but one continuous track. If you didn't have an answer for either of my previous questions, these seven pursuits will give you direction and clarity so that regardless of what you do or become, you'll live a life pleasing to the Lord and full of meaningful service for his kingdom.

Perhaps you have a solid sense of what you want to do and which direction you'll go. As you read, consider whether those ambitions align with the seven pursuits I've outlined here. If so, I'm confident you'll flourish as a follower of Jesus in whatever you do. If your pursuits are fundamentally at odds with the principles that follow, I'm hopeful you'll pause to reevaluate your course.

In the end, maybe you'll discover a new dream for how you can serve God's kingdom—something you never envisioned before. When you do, I pray you will *make it your ambition*.

1

Make It Your Ambition to Know and Love God

What's the biggest, most significant, single most important thing you could spend your life pursuing? This question is one that philosophers, wisdom seekers, artists, politicians, rulers, teachers, and *everyone* has asked for thousands of years. Apart from the question of the meaning of life, which is similar but different, this question is The Big One for human beings. We all innately need to know that what we do matters—that we each have a significant contribution to make in this world.

Naturally, I asked a robot in our rapidly advancing AI systems to find the answer. Because, you know, robots on the internet would undoubtedly know the answer to life's biggest questions. Here's what AI summarized: "The pursuit of a fulfilling life is a deeply personal journey, and what constitutes the 'greatest' thing to pursue can vary from person to person."[1]

Great! Even the robots don't know how to answer The Big One for the human race (it's probably because they know we won't need them anymore if they tell us, and the human race will have thwarted their plans for world domination).

All joking aside, AI couldn't give a definitive answer, but it did provide a few suggestions. It highlighted pursuits like happiness, fulfillment, and embracing new opportunities. It posited finding true love as another option for the most significant thing a person could pursue. Social media also works hard to convince us that a life of exploration, adventure, and world travel would be a pinnacle pursuit to give life meaning and purpose.

Ultimate Pursuit

Thankfully, God's Word also keys in on this question. Tucked in the middle of the Bible is a wild book of Hebrew wisdom poetry called Ecclesiastes, authored by "the Preacher," who identifies himself as the son of David, king in Jerusalem (Eccl. 1:1). At the outset, he has a gloomy outlook on the meaning and pursuits of life. He's a melancholy guy, saying that everything in life is "vanity," or empty and meaningless. "Everything is meaningless," he declares (v. 2, NIV). When the Preacher tries to tackle the question of life's greatest pursuit, his answer doesn't seem much better than AI's attempt. However,

1. Response to "What is the greatest thing I could spend my life pursuing?" Microsoft Copilot, March 1, 2024, edited for style and accuracy.

this king (likely Solomon) has unlimited resources and can try a handful of paths. He tries to gain philosophical wisdom and concludes, "He who increases in knowledge increases sorrow" (v. 18). He makes a run at gaining as much pleasure as possible. He also acquires great wealth and prominence: "Whatever my eyes desired I did not keep from them" (2:10). Those pursuits ended up being empty and meaningless as well. He pivoted to hard work, building great monuments and gardens and parks, thinking that creating an impressive legacy would be a life worth living. This attempt, too, turned out depressing because he realized he'd spend his whole life working and striving only for someone else to enjoy the reward of it all (vv. 18–19).

His conclusion after these experiments was this: "I perceived that there is nothing better for [people] than to be joyful and to do good as long as they live; also that everyone should eat and drink and take pleasure in all his toil—this is God's gift to man" (3:12–13). Wow. That's it? Eat a great steak with a glass of fine wine and have a job you enjoy. *That's* the Bible's answer to the question about the greatest pursuit a human being can have in his life? If this is all the Bible says about our greatest pursuits, then this book should be very short.

At this point, AI is saying, "I have no clue, but I hope you enjoy life," and the Preacher is recommending, "Eat good food, drink good drinks, and enjoy your job." Maybe we should lower our expectations for our life pursuits and just try to have a good time. Frankly, some have already done that. But our inquiries here have left a third person out of the conversation. Because if the robots and the ancient king who has the most can't give clear answers to the greatest pursuit of life, who can?

The point of the Preacher's entire work is that everything "under the sun" (everything this world offers apart from God) is empty and meaningless. In the grand picture, what pursuits are worthwhile without God? A good meal? Pleasure? Your job? Yet, as the Preacher contends, a person who remembers "[his] Creator in the days of [his] youth" (12:1) or a person who fears God and "keeps his commandments" (v. 13) is a person living with a greater trajectory in his life. These two statements are a way of saying that the single most important thing you could spend your life pursuing is God.

I'd like to say it like this: *The greatest ambition you can have for your life is to know and love God*. While other ambitions may be good and worthwhile, every other pursuit is subordinate to this ultimate undertaking.

In case you don't want to take my word for it—or the Preacher's word, for that matter—let me show you a few other places in the Bible where this is highlighted as the prime ambition for the life of every believer.

Toward the end of Jesus's ministry, before his death on the cross, several religious groups in Israel were trying to find a reason to discredit Jesus and his teachings. One sect in particular, the Sadducees, thought they could find fault with him by bringing an expert lawyer to test Jesus on matters of Jewish law. So the lawyer asked Jesus, "Teacher, which is the great commandment in the Law?" (Matt. 22:36). Now, Jesus not only had to sift through the Ten Commandments to find one to rank highest but also had to navigate through more than 600 additional commandments found in the Old Testament writings. How would he pick the winner out of all those?

Jesus didn't need time to think. His answer was both brilliant and clarifying: "He said to him, 'You shall love the Lord your God with all your heart and with all your soul and with all your mind. This is the great and first commandment'" (vv. 37–38). There it is. The highest or greatest and most important thing a human being should do is love God.

In an earlier sermon (Jesus was a preacher, after all), he'd talked about the things that make us anxious or keep us awake at night: concerns about our next meal, what we'll wear, and the troubles that tomorrow could potentially bring. As he identified those anxieties, he dared to tell us not to be anxious about these things. He said, "For the Gentiles [i.e., people who live apart from God] seek after all these things, and your heavenly Father knows that you need them all" (6:32). Jesus is reassuring us that God knows we need the food and clothes that make up our day-to-day existence. And he's promising to take care of us.

Clarifying the Goal

Instead of staying preoccupied with these worries, we're called by Jesus to aim at a higher pursuit: "But seek first the kingdom of God and his righteousness, and all these things will be added to you" (v. 33). Jesus here tells us to have the highest and greatest priority built around seeking God's kingdom and his righteousness. When I talk about God's kingdom, I'm referring the ever-expanding realm here on earth where God's rule and reign is honored and upheld. God's kingdom isn't a place on earth today, but God's rule is made known by the community of people who know and love God. Therefore, Jesus is saying the greatest pursuit we should have is to know and love God, to seek more and more to know and love him well.

Another person who affirms this pursuit is the apostle Paul. If you know his story, you know he was a pretty ambitious guy. He wanted to be the top of his class, the best in his field. Furthermore, he was zealous to ensure he stood head and shoulders above everyone else in life. But then a stunning thing happened. In an undeniable way, he was confronted with the reality that Jesus Christ died for our sins, was raised to life again on the third day, and is Lord and Savior. Paul's ambition completely changed.

In a letter to a church he'd planted, Paul tells the believers to look out for false teachers and those who want to depend on their own righteous deeds as valid sources of salvation. They're entirely wrong, he says, and he can prove it by his own life.

> If anyone else thinks he has reason for confidence in the flesh, I have more: circumcised on the eighth day, of the people of Israel, of the tribe of Benjamin, a Hebrew of Hebrews; as to the law, a Pharisee; as to zeal, a persecutor of the church; as to righteousness under the law, blameless. But whatever gain I had, I counted as loss for the sake of Christ. Indeed, I count everything as loss because of *the surpassing worth of knowing Christ Jesus my Lord*. (Phil. 3:4–8, emphasis added)

According to Paul, nothing in life matches up to or has greater value than knowing Christ. You can feel it as he tells the Philippians what his life is aimed at: "[To] gain Christ and be found in him . . . that *I may know him* and the power of his resurrection" (vv. 8–10, emphasis added). Knowing Christ is a matter of greatest value and highest worth.

When I listen to the collective wisdom of Jesus, Paul, and others in the Bible, it becomes evident that knowing and loving God is the greatest ambition a person can have for his or her life. One of the most monumental educational writings about the Christian faith, the Westminster Shorter Catechism, begins by asking, "What is the chief end of man?" The answer? "Man's chief end is to glorify God, and enjoy him forever."[2] Our spiritual ancestors affirm that living to know and love God is the best pursuit of a person's life. J. I. Packer, whose book *Knowing God* had a tremendous influence on my life, says, "Disregard [knowing] God, and you sentence yourself to stumble and blunder through life blindfolded, as it were, with no sense of direction and no understanding of what surrounds you. This way you can waste your life and lose your soul."[3]

The greatest ambition you can have is to know and love God.

What Does It Mean to Know and Love God?

But what does knowing and loving God mean in everyday life? It's a big aspiration, but how can we truly know

2. R. C. Sproul, ed., "The Westminster Shorter Catechism," in *The Reformation Study Bible: English Standard Version* (Reformation Trust, 2015), 2471–77.
3. J. I. Packer, *Knowing God* (IVP, 2023), 19.

God, let alone love him with all our heart, soul, mind, and body? It may seem overly simplistic on my part, but here's the truth: You know and love God by relating to him as you would to another person, through the skills of building a relationship and friendship.

Think about what it means to cultivate a friendship with another person. You get to know things about him: his favorite hobbies and meals, what he's afraid of, what his ideal vacation is, and other details of his everyday life. But knowing someone involves knowing more than what he does or doesn't like. Many today talk about being known as "being seen." In a way, knowing and loving God is all about seeing, discerning, and relating to who he is.

To know God involves more than knowing theological propositions, such as the fact that God is holy. It requires comprehending and seeing how his holiness is expressed in the world. Someone who lives to know God considers how God's holiness intersects and gives shape to her own life. In a way, knowing another person is dancing with him or her. You must be aware of the directions and steps of movement the other person will take with you as you sway and move to the music. The best dancers get close, eyes locked on each other. They can discern the body language, postures, and movements that produce a beautiful and enjoyable expression of art set to music. When the dancers don't know one another or the steps of the dance, they can end up stepping on and tripping over each other, to their embarrassment.

The way these dancers get good is through time and intentional practice with each other. The same is true for us in knowing God. The practices, or habits, of spiritual growth with God are time-tested means by which we can seek to know him better. Let me share a few of these vital habits. First, daily reading and intake of the Bible will help you know God's character, his will, his ways, and his work in the world and in your life. The Bible is where God has chosen to reveal himself, so you can't know anything about him objectively apart from immersing yourself in the Scriptures. Along with Bible reading, regular prayer helps you commune and speak with God regarding the issues of your heart and life and of the world. Jesus encourages us to regularly pray, to seek our Father in heaven and express our dependence on and need of him for all of life (Matt. 6:5–15). A third vital habit is worshiping God with a local church. By weekly participating in worship services where the Bible is taught, the ordinances (or sacraments) are observed, and the church sings to God, we grow as a community in knowing God together. Spiritual leaders instruct and encourage us in areas of our lives we might never evaluate if left to ourselves. We find the ability to express generosity, care, and love toward one another and those outside the faith. These spiritual habits are essential practices to help us learn the dance of knowing and loving God well.

Knowing and loving God means we understand his character (who he is) and his activity in the universe (what he's doing). But it also means having an affection or desire for God. To know and love God means an inclination in your heart increasingly grows in approval, happiness, joy, eagerness, and pleasure in God. You could describe this as *enjoying God*, which is why, I believe, the authors of the previously mentioned Westminster

Shorter Catechism included both knowing and enjoying as the chief goal of our lives.

When I first met Stephanie, I wasn't sure if we'd be friends, let alone husband and wife. I was in a season of significant transition and had gone to visit my elderly grandparents for a week to help them pack and move from their farmhouse to a smaller, more manageable residence closer to town. Within the first hour after I arrived, my grandmother told me about a woman in her Sunday school class at church who she was sure was "the one" for me. I resisted my grandmother's attempts to play matchmaker right from the start. Eventually, her persistence (and meddling) won out. I ended up meeting Stephanie and taking her out on a date. Except she didn't know it was a date. My grandmother had asked her to hang out with me so I wouldn't have to be around "old people" the entire time I was visiting. As our "date" was wrapping up, I boldly asked Stephanie what she thought about a long-distance relationship. (After all, I was planning to live in a different state.) In response, she chuckled and replied, "I don't." Looking back, she was pretty clear, but I'm not the quickest to pick up signals. So I asked her later that week to have dinner again ("date" number two). As we talked, I brought long-distance dating up again, and once again she laughed. It seemed our relationship would amount to nothing more than being acquaintances.

Yet we continued to spend time together and get to know each other. Knowing things about each other turned into knowing and seeing the other person. We discovered shared affinities and shared longings for our lives, and the dance of our lives together soon found a rhythm and cadence of mutual delight. I enjoyed being with her. She enjoyed being with me. After a while, we couldn't envision our lives without one other. We came to love each other. Twenty-plus years later, we've cultivated a much deeper, more intimate, and more profound relationship. We know each other so much better, have greater and more intense affection for each other, and enjoy our life together. We often take up a borrowed line from Wendell Berry when we write notes to each other, saying, "Let's live right on."[4] I still can't envision her not being part of my life.

Could you say that same thing or begin to envision that kind of relational life with God? Do you know him, enjoy him, or even desire him to be your life's greatest, highest, and best relationship? If you're going to live with your sights set on the most significant and biggest ambition in the universe, you must pursue knowing and loving God. You must build a relationship of friendship and intimacy with him.

Why Should I Live to Know and Love God?

Here's where you might ask another big question: "Why?" When we evaluate all that we chase and pursue in our lives, does knowing and loving God really need to be the greatest passion? Let me answer this question with four reasons that have motivated me to make this my ambition. These reasons stem from the deeper reality that God has loved me first (1 John 4:10, 19). When you and I realize we deserve nothing good but only God's

4. Wendell Berry, *Hannah Coulter* (Shoemaker & Hoard, 2005), 141.

wrath for our sin, and then we see that God loved us in the greatest way and gave his Son for us to forgive us (Gal. 1:3–5), we're made alive to love him. Our seeking to know and love God is never rightly an attempt to earn God's love. He's already shown his love for us in Christ. We respond to his love with love ourselves.

The first reason is found in understanding God's purposes for creating the entire universe. In one powerful statement in Romans 11, Paul summarizes the scope of God's purpose for creating everything, including human beings: "For from him and through him and to him are all things. To him be glory forever" (v. 36). The entire arc of our existence is summed up in the prepositions. We were created by or *from* God. We live and have our very existence *through* God. Our aim or highest purpose is *to* God, and the result is "to him be glory forever." The best way we can live to glorify God is to know and love him with our lives. That's the very purpose for which we were created.

Second, knowing and loving God has continuous eternal value. Remember our friend the Preacher and his wisdom in Ecclesiastes? He reflects that God has "set eternity in the human heart" (3:11, NIV). By that, he means we were made for eternity and God has put eternal desires and pursuits into our hearts. The problem is that nothing this world offers us is eternally valuable and lasting. We won't take any possessions with us when we die. The things we spend our careers building end up obsolete or torn down. We all grow old and die. But if we live to know and love God, we'll live for something beyond death. A glorious and satisfying future awaits those who know and love God.

Third, and this is closely related to the last reason, we can never fully exhaust knowing or loving God, and those who make it their ambition to know and love him will never get bored in this pursuit. Consider this: All we can possibly know about God *at this moment* is given in the pages of Scripture. Yet there's a vast and wide "unsearchableness" to God; we'll have forever to pursue him. David declares, "Great is the Lord and most worthy of praise; his greatness no one can fathom" (Ps. 145:3, NIV). A fathom is an old style of measurement mainly used to describe the ocean's depths. The idea here is that you can't measure out how great God is. Yet Paul prays in Ephesians 3:18–19 that we might have "strength to comprehend with all the saints what is the breadth and length and height and depth, and to know the love of Christ that surpasses knowledge, that [we] may be filled with all the fullness of God." If we make this our great ambition, you and I will have *forever* to know and love someone who will take *forever* to comprehend.

Last, making it our ambition to know and love God in this life provides the greatest hope for us amid the world's deep brokenness and fallenness. Let's be honest: Things aren't exactly wonderful at this stage of human history. The world around us is fractured and eroding. Life in a broken world can make us feel the same despair as the Preacher, who looked at life "under the sun" apart from God and rightly said, "Everything is meaningless" (Eccl. 1:2, NIV). But if we live to know and love God, who's working to make all things new, we have a greater purpose and story to live within. We can make sense of our suffering and trials as well as have peace and hope for the future. As Packer said, "Once you become aware that the main business that you are here for is to know God, most of life's problems fall into place of their own accord."[5]

Living with the highest ambition to know and love God gives us trajectory, perspective, purpose, and hope for our lives right here and now. Whether we live to be 100 years old or don't even make it to 50, life will be complete if we know and love God.

How Is a Growing Relationship with God Possible?

How can we orient our lives around this incredible ambition and purpose? If you remember my encouragement about how to build relationships with people, then you'll see glimpses of the pattern I'm laying out. You must build a relationship of friendship and intimacy with God.

Yet even that statement contains a massive problem. We're natively enemies with God. The Bible describes all human beings as estranged from God, lost, and dead in our trespasses and sins (Ps. 58:3; Luke 19:10; Eph. 2:1). We're enemies of his and "by nature children of wrath" (Eph. 2:3). So purposing to grow in a friendship with God seems entirely off the table unless there is some kind of reconciliation and restoration. To make matters worse, we're incapable of reconciling and restoring the relationship ourselves. What could a spiritually dead, corrupt-at-the-core, hostile-to-God person do to make it all right?

Nothing.

5. Packer, *Knowing God*, 34.

Yep, you read that correctly. There's not a thing we can do to reconcile ourselves with God.

But don't let that bother you, because the really good news is that God has done *everything* to reconcile us to himself. He's identified the problem of our hearts: our sin (Rom. 3:23). He's weighed out the penalty of our rebellion: death (6:23). He's considered that to reconcile us justly to himself, his eternal justice must be satisfied and humanity's penalty must be paid (3:25–26). The eternal son of God, Jesus Christ, was made human. He is the God-man (Phil. 2:5–8). Jesus came and lived without sin in order to fulfill the required righteousness of God (2 Cor. 5:21). And Jesus stood as a substitute sacrifice for us and died on the cross to pay our penalty of sin (Isa. 53:4–6). Furthermore, on the third day, he arose from the dead—defeating sin, giving righteousness to everyone who believes, and securing a reconciled relationship with him forever (Rom. 1:3–4; 5:19; Eph. 2:5–7).

The relationship of friendship and intimacy with God begins when we acknowledge our sins and then turn in faith to Jesus and place our trust in him as the only One who rescues and reconciles us through his perfect life, atoning death, and bodily resurrection. As Tim Keller says, "The gospel is this: We are more sinful and flawed in ourselves than we ever dared believe, yet at the very same time we are more loved and accepted in Jesus Christ than we ever dared hope."[6]

6. Timothy Keller and Kathy Keller, *The Meaning of Marriage: Facing the Complexities of Commitment with the Wisdom of God*, 1st ed. (Dutton, 2011), 48.

It's on the basis of this good news that our lives really begin; they are really made new. From what Jesus did for us, a reconciled relationship with God allows us to get to know him better, love him more, discern his will, enjoy his presence, and experience every good and perfect gift he has waiting for his people. From this starting point, we should make it the ambition of our lives to know and love God forever.

There's a profound invitation in C. S. Lewis's last volume in the *Chronicles of Narnia* series, *The Last Battle*. Children from the earlier volumes—Peter, Lucy, Edmund, Eustace, Jill, Digory, and Polly—enter into a new world that stuns their senses. They cannot pinpoint why the new world feels so familiar yet staggeringly distinct. That is, until the unicorn Jewel has the insight that they are, in fact, in the real Narnia. They've left the "Shadowlands" behind and are in for an eternity of discovery and delight. With the exciting revelation of this new land, with all its beauty and endless discoveries to be made, Jewel repeatedly gives the invitation to go "further up and further in" as they make endless beautiful discoveries.[7]

This is the invitation to a life aimed at knowing and loving God. Further up and further in, there's more of God to know. Further up and further in, there's more of God to love. Further up and further in, you were made to know him. Further up and further in, endless beauty and glory await. Further up and further in, you'll forever be satisfied. Christ invites us to an inexhaustible universe of discovery of his glory and grace. Let's start our lives

7. C. S. Lewis, *The Last Battle*, 1st Harper Trophy ed., *The Chronicles of Narnia*, bk. 7 (HarperTrophy, 2000), 196ff.

today with the ambition of knowing and loving God. Further up and further in!

Discussion Questions

1. What would you say is the most significant thing a human being could spend his or her life pursuing?
2. How does the statement "The greatest ambition you can have for your life is to know and love God" agree or disagree with your perspective of life?
3. Is knowing and loving God something you're practically pursuing? What means or habits of spiritual growth do you need to pick up to know God?
4. How does what Christ did in his life, death, and resurrection make knowing and loving God possible?
5. What would your life look like if you made this first pursuit your greatest ambition?

2

Make It Your Ambition to Model Christ's Character

You're dead.

You can come up with the details of how and when. Your imagination can decide if you lived a long life or a brief one and whether it was cancer that took you or a tragic accident. I'll let you color in those details. But I get to tell you about your funeral.

People show up who knew you in one capacity or another. Not as many come as you had hoped or would expect, but it's more than just a few. Some of the folks really liked you; a small handful loved you. The rest are there out of obligation and decency.

A pastor you don't know stands up to deliver a eulogy, but you can tell he's struggling with what to say. He tells the congregation the data about your life: when you were born and when you died. He names the one or two relatives you left behind. He talks about the work you did and the jobs you held. As you listen to him, you get the sense he doesn't know you. And you'd be right. Whoever was responsible for making arrangements called around several churches, and this officiant was the only one willing to handle the service.

At one point during your brief funeral, the pastor offers an opportunity for people to share memories about you. A few coworkers stand up and try to lighten the mood by telling a story about a joke you told once. The retelling gets a few chuckles. They talk about your work and what you were like as a coworker. Adjectives like "driven," "committed," and "smart" were used. They spoke favorably of the job you did, and the integrity you showed in your work. You lived a decent life.

One of your college roommates stands up to talk about you. They share how devoted you were to your studies, how eager you were to earn a great internship, and then advance through your career with all the trappings of success. Again, more adjectives describe how you went about life and your pursuit of your career goals.

After a little less than an hour, the service concludes, and everyone departs. And with that, the sum total of honor given to your life is completed. *Maybe* 45 minutes spent reviewing what could be compared to a résumé.[1] The "celebration of life" ceremony thrown for you doesn't feel like a party, nor does the life it tried to honor

1. See David Brooks's distinction between résumé and eulogy values: David Brooks, "Should You Live for Your Résumé . . . or Your Eulogy?" TED Talk, Vancouver, BC, March 2014, https://www.ted.com/talks/david_brooks_should_you_live_for_your_resume_or_your_eulogy.

seem like a full life. No lasting influence. It's all boring and seemingly wasted.

Is that what you hope your life will amount to? Is the legacy you hope to leave bound up in the career you enter and the work you accomplish?

Who Are You Becoming?

Here's why I shared this potential future with you: I want you to think about what kind of person you're becoming and who you'll be. The Preacher from Ecclesiastes declared, "It is better to go to a house of mourning than to go to a house of feasting, for death is the destiny of everyone; the living should take this to heart" (Eccl. 7:2, NIV). Funerals get us to think about our end and the legacy we'll leave. If they're honest, funerals are where the essence of a person's character is rehearsed. What do you think will be said (or thought) about you at your funeral?

In the light of your future funeral, I want to put before you a second life pursuit. Here and now, even today, *make it your ambition to possess and model the character of Christ*. Make it your ambition to be like Christ.

Before I talk about how to get there and what it even looks like to imitate Christ, I want to encourage you. It may seem daunting and aggressively ambitious to pick the one person in human history who was perfect and say, "Be like him!" We know ourselves and others well enough to admit nobody is perfect. This could sound like a setup for failure right at the onset. Am I putting you on a path of disappointment and discouragement from the beginning?

No, that's not my goal at all. It's in light of *who you will be* that I want to encourage you to pursue being like Christ today. Let me draw out a few realities the Bible gives us regarding who we are and who we will be on the ultimate last day. The apostle John says to Jesus's followers (I assume you're one too), "Beloved, we are God's children now, and what we will be has not yet appeared; but we know that when he appears we shall be like him, because we shall see him as he is. And everyone who thus hopes in him purifies himself as he is pure" (1 John 3:2–3).

You Will Become like Jesus

First, John anchors believers in an absolute identity: "We are God's children now." This identity stands on the good news I shared in the last chapter. Being reconciled to God by Jesus Christ's blood means you belong to God as his adopted child. Your identity is firmly established, and God doesn't lose or give up on any of his children (John 10:28–29). You're his beloved child, completely affirmed and secure in him. That's really good news!

Next, John looks forward to who we will become. He says, "What we will be has not yet appeared," or to say it another way, what we will be has not yet been revealed. Christians have speculated and wondered for centuries what our bodies will look like and be like when Jesus comes again. John's answer is "Who knows?"

Yet there is something we can be sure of. We do know that "when [Christ] appears we shall be like him, because we shall see him as he is." Our future is that we who are believers in Jesus Christ will be *like Jesus*. Every one of his followers will get that long-awaited glimpse of the resurrected Jesus, and we'll be immediately and completely transformed to be like him. We'll be perfect, just as he is perfect.

If that's your future in Christ—being fully and completely perfect just as he is—what does it mean for your life today? Some will be inclined to ask, "What does it matter how I live now? I can be whoever I want and live however I'd like, and it will all get sorted out in the end. Why try to be like Jesus today if doing that will just end up in failure, guilt, and shame? I'll just wait until I see Jesus, and it'll all be fine." John has one more comment that answers this thinking. He says, "Everyone who thus hopes in [Jesus] purifies himself as he is pure" (1 John 3:3). Everyone who banks her life on Jesus is actively living to become like him. To possess the goal of our faith means we'll *pursue* the goal of our faith.

I hope you see it here. John tells us who we are (children of God), what we will become (like Jesus), and how to get there (purifying ourselves as he is pure). For me to challenge you to make it your ambition to possess and model Christ's character isn't setting the bar too high; it's setting the bar precisely where it should be. You were redeemed and rescued by Christ's blood to be like Christ. *The ambition is to become who you've already been saved to be.*

Understand the Character of Christ

What then does it look like to possess and model Christ's character? If we're going to be like Jesus, how would we classify or speak about his character?

I find lists helpful. They give me a sense of order and cohesion. Some of my lists are of books I'd like to read, and others are of projects and tasks I need to accomplish and complete (this little book was one of those tasks on a list somewhere).

Some lists break down the steps for completing one larger task. I'm thinking of this kind of list as we talk about Christ's character. If we could draw up a list of specific character qualities or virtues of Jesus, that would help us identify more precisely the virtues we seek to possess. Paul gives us a clear, though not exhaustive, list in Galatians 5 of the virtues that should mark the life of a believer seeking to emulate Christ. We know them as the fruit of the Spirit.

This list of Christian virtues is the opposite of what we could live out on our own. In fact, what we're capable of on our own shows up in a separate list, describing the "works of the flesh":

> Now the works of the flesh are evident: sexual immorality, impurity, sensuality, idolatry, sorcery, enmity, strife, jealousy, fits of anger, rivalries, dissensions, divisions, envy, drunkenness, orgies, and things like these. I warn you, as I warned you before, that those who do such things will not inherit the kingdom of God. (Gal. 5:19–21)

That's a staggering list—the kind that would reflect villain status in most contexts. A person who lacks Christ's character is a quick-tempered, violent, self-absorbed, sensual, divisive, undisciplined "me-monster"[2] of a person. Paul warns that a person of this wicked character is

2. Thanks to Brian Regan for coining that term.

most likely not a true disciple of Jesus and therefore will not enter his kingdom.

By contrast, the fruit of the Spirit we just mentioned is evidence of the Spirit of Jesus at work in my life. Jesus is the total and complete expression of each of these characteristics:

> The fruit of the Spirit is love, joy, peace, patience, kindness, goodness, faithfulness, gentleness, self-control; against such things there is no law. And those who belong to Christ Jesus have crucified the flesh with its passions and desires. If we live by the Spirit, let us also keep in step with the Spirit. (Gal. 5:22–25)

Compare this list to how Jesus lived and acted as recorded in the Gospels, and you won't find any discrepancies.

Maybe we should envision this not merely as a list but as a syllabus. If we're going to become like Jesus, this is the scope and sequence of our character development. From now until you see Jesus face-to-face, you're enrolled in The University of Christian Character (The U!). As you more deeply understand Christ's work on your behalf and how your heart has been transferred from spiritual death to life, you invite the Spirit to continue working repentance and faith in your heart. The fruit of love, joy, peace, patience, kindness, goodness, faithfulness, gentleness, and self-control is increasingly evident in our lives as we grow to love Jesus more.

Experientially, you explore the practical labs of self-denial, fighting sin, and suffering. The U's athletic program, which is compulsory, trains every student in synchronized walking with the Holy Spirit. To possess

Christ's character, you must know him more deeply and surrender to his work in your life.

Take a look at this "course list" for a moment. Does this help identify the places where your character needs development? Are there some "classes" you've yet to take? Could you look at your life and say, "I'm loving other people in just the ways that Jesus loved others"? Is the same gentleness that Jesus possessed and displayed also modeled in your life? How are you doing regarding self-control?

Here's why I put out a list or syllabus like this for us—it's a biblical description of the life of a growing disciple of Jesus. When the writer of Hebrews said, "Strive for . . . the holiness without which no one will see the Lord" (12:14), we have an abstract idea in our minds about holiness. But does holiness mean not watching movies, drinking alcohol, or dancing? Or does it mean something else, something more? Instead of defining holiness by what we do or don't do, we can look at Jesus and assess his character and the qualities of his virtue alongside a list like the fruit of the Spirit—and holiness becomes more concrete. Love is holiness; patience is holiness; goodness is holiness. Jesus perfectly embodied every one of these qualities, and because of this, we must let him live his life through us as we seek to grow in Christlikeness.

Imitate Christ

Practically, let's discuss what this means. How do we grow in Christlikeness? How does someone become proficient in just about anything he or she does? Usually, it takes years of training, lots of instruction, careful attention to the details, and effort to get there. Developing Christian character is like becoming a master sushi chef (or *itamae*).

In Japan, becoming an *itamae* isn't an overnight process. It takes decades to reach the ability and proficiency of a master *itamae* and open your own sushi bar. The apprentice will do the tedious chores of cleaning the shop, washing the dishes, and other tasks that have nothing to do with fish, rice, or knives. After some time (maybe as long as five years), the apprentice gets to move closer to the master and learn the rice preparation. Again, this skill takes years to learn under the tutelage of the *itamae*. Mastering the technique requires careful attention and mimicry of the master chef. Once the master sees the apprentice has fully imitated the skill, the apprentice is invited to be a *wakiita*, someone who stands next to the cutting board. At the side of the master chef, the *wakiita* apprentice learns the knife skills required to clean the various types of fish and shellfish. He learns the master's movements and motions, how he cuts pieces of fish and builds the *nigiri* just right. Finally, after many long years of repetition and discipline, the apprentice is given the *itamae* title and allowed to stand in front of the cutting board as a superior chef.[3]

While no one will master being like Christ in this life, we can and should pursue apprenticeship under Jesus. It will take the rest of our lives, and even our death, to

3. "Sushi Chef Apprentice," Mrs. Lin's Kitchen, August 2009, https://www.mrslinskitchen.com/nlaug09.html. The documentary film *Jiro Dreams of Sushi* (Magnolia Picture, 2012) also shows the life of one of the most renowned *itamaes* in Japan.

bring us into complete Christlikeness and character. Yet there's still room to grow and for character to develop in our lives here and now. Let me suggest three practices that will help you move forward in becoming like Christ.

Three Practices for Growing in Christ

First, *meditate*. I don't mean the kind of meditation practiced in Eastern religions that involves emptying your mind and getting to a place of internal stillness where there are no thoughts, only tranquility and Zen. I mean for you to take hold of truth, specifically Scripture, and mull over and chew on it. To be an apprentice of master Jesus, you must "watch" him. Open the Bible and begin reading about Jesus and his life. Think about how he talked to people. Observe how he behaved in various situations. Ask why he spoke the way he did. Consider how he responded to religious leaders and then how he responded to obvious sinners. What traits and characteristics from the fruit of the Spirit list does he display when he's questioned and challenged? Ponder and meditate on Jesus's life. As you reflect on the character of God in Jesus Christ, begin to look at your own life as well. Why do you respond differently than Jesus does in certain situations? Where do you not align with Jesus's character in your thoughts, attitudes, desires, and behavior?

When you meditate on Christ and realize the gap in your own lifestyle, you can pick up the next practice for becoming like Christ: *mortify*. I don't mean mortify as in frighten or embarrass. I mean mortify in the old way, to subdue or kill. Paul talked about mortifying our flesh (the sinful nature and desires within us) by saying,

"Those who belong to Christ Jesus have *crucified* the flesh with its passions and desires" (Gal. 5:24, emphasis added). Or, in another place, Paul says to "put to death . . . whatever belongs to your earthly nature: sexual immorality, impurity, lust, evil desires and greed, which is idolatry" (Col. 3:5, NIV). The idea of mortifying your flesh is to identify and confess sin and let the Spirit subdue your sinful heart. Mortification is an ongoing discipline of deliberately choosing to honor and obey Christ and saying no to our hearts' sinful and foolish desires. As you, by the Spirit's power, go to battle against your flesh, you'll find your affections and desires *for* God grow as well.

In some ways, mortification is similar to working out and getting physically fit. You subject your body to strenuous cardio and strength training, regularly attending the gym and going through the exercise program. You eat a healthy diet and cut out the sweets and carbs that add on the pounds (even though they taste *really* good). You reject your desires and expend effort to be stronger, fitter, and more in shape. Growing in the character of Christ is a means of self-discipline to become like him by not indulging in and practicing the deeds of your flesh. In his power that works within you (Col. 1:29), you go to battle against your sin.

The third practice to pick up, along with meditating and mortifying, is to *mimic*. Another way of saying this is to imitate. By mimicking or imitating, you're trying to observe and duplicate another person's way of life. Specifically, I'm encouraging you to imitate Jesus Christ. Consider the behaviors you observed as you meditated on Jesus's life, then try them on yourself. Did Jesus express love toward hostile people? You follow him in that behavior. Did Jesus demonstrate humility and patience toward difficult people? You give it a try. Imitate Jesus Christ's character in your own life and practice.

How do we know what Jesus would do in all the granular, everyday things? In addition to everything we've discussed about a growing affection for and surrender to Christ, we must also have close relationships with others who are following Jesus. Paul invited the believers in Corinth to imitate him as he imitates Christ (1 Cor. 11:1, CSB). He encouraged the Philippian believers, "Join in imitating me, and keep your eyes on those who walk according to the example you have in us" (Phil. 3:17). The writer of Hebrews challenges us to "remember your leaders, those who spoke to you the word of God. Consider the outcome of their way of life and *imitate* their faith" (Heb. 13:7, emphasis added). We're encouraged to follow and get close to other Christians and mimic their lifestyle and faith as they follow Jesus Christ. You'll be wise to have an older, faithful believer in your life who pursues Christ's character and mentors you. This is what discipleship is: being an apprentice of master Jesus and imitating his life.

Make Character Your Ambition

Let me conclude this chapter back where I started. You're dead. Or you will be one day. In light of that coming day, who are you *becoming* now? Will the legacy you leave consist mostly of the work you did? Or will something greater be said about you? Will people talk about who you became, the character and the virtue that you exhibited faithfully through your life? This better legacy can be yours! Christ has obtained it for everyone who has put their hope in him. If that's true of you, can you seek every day to become more like him? Yes, it will take effort. You need godly role models and mentors to give you an embodied vision of what Christ's character looks like. But you can make progress in becoming like Christ. Don Carson is right: "People do not drift toward holiness. Apart from grace-driven effort, people do not gravitate toward godliness, prayer, obedience to Scripture, faith, and delight in the Lord."[4] This is why we must make growing in Christlike character a main pursuit of our lives.

Will you take up this pursuit? Will you consider your enrollment in The University of Christian Character, examine the syllabus, and begin the program of a lifelong apprenticeship under Jesus? Many believers in my generation and my parents' generation have sacrificed character on the altar of politics, wealth, and worldly status. When we do this, we trade holiness for hostility, integrity for influence, patience for power, and virtue for victories. To the degree we reject the way of Jesus, we waste our lives.

I can hardly imagine what the world would be like if *your* generation of Christians would make character their life pursuit. How much would the world be changed and the gospel of Jesus adorned if there was a movement of holiness among young adults today? What if your generation committed, at all costs, to love Jesus more deeply and to embody the humble, extraordinary,

4. D. A. Carson, *For the Love of God: A Daily Companion for Discovering the Riches of God's Word*, vol. 2, (Crossway, 1998), 49.

compassionate, compelling love of God in Jesus Christ? The legacy your generation could leave would be felt across not only decades but centuries. That movement starts with you. Make it your ambition to model the character of your Savior, Jesus.

Discussion Questions

1. What do you think will be said (or thought) about you at your funeral? Will you be perceived well or seen as a villain?
2. How does knowing the Christian's certain future of being made perfectly like Christ encourage us in pursuing Christlikeness today?
3. Contrast the list of the "works of the flesh" (Gal. 5:19–21) and the "fruit of the Spirit" (vv. 22–25). What do you notice about your own character in light of these two lists? Which one describes your heart and behaviors?
4. Which of the three practices of imitating Christ are needed in your life right now?
5. What would your life look like if you made it your ambition to model Christ's character?

3

Make It Your Ambition to Discern, Develop, and Deploy Your Gifts

Jacob is a musician. He hears melodies and harmonies in his head that he can bring to life on the keys and synthesizers he works with. He's learned to play piano and guitar and even keep the beat on the drum kit. As a band leader, he works to help his band members perform at their highest potential and make excellent music. He's creative in thinking about how to articulate things he's passionate about as he composes song lyrics.

Marsha is an accountant. Her mind works in numbers and formulas. She's detail-oriented and able to keep track of large amounts of money, managing it faithfully down to the penny. She can forecast, categorize, and report her organization's cash flow so it can pay its bills and function optimally. Her knowledge of financial regulations and procedures keeps her organization operating well within the scope of the law, and the organization doesn't fear embezzlement or significant loss.

Erin is a teacher. She can break down complex ideas and concepts and make them understandable and attainable for 10-year-olds. She is skilled in using various techniques and educational philosophies to speak to the different learning styles of the children in her classroom. She's a warm, caring person who understands that education is more than just giving students information; it involves engaging all their faculties. She continues learning about the subjects she teaches to stay sharp and develop the most effective ways to lead students.

Clayton is a general contractor. With what seems like only a hammer and nails, he can manufacture everything from a standing garden to an entire home. He knows the right kinds of material to use, where to lay foundations, how to plumb and how to pull electrical wires, and everything else that goes into constructing and maintaining a building. He's up to date on the latest and safest building codes in his community so that if there were any personal or property injuries, the damage would be limited. The building projects he oversees are highly sought after and renowned for their quality.

These four people have a great diversity of skill sets, education, and experience. Yet each is pursuing mastery and a high level of competency in his or her occupation. We can't imagine Jacob stepping into Marsha's office and effectively picking up her job. Nor do we see Clayton sitting down with Erin's 10-year-olds to instruct them in social studies and writing a formal book report. Thankfully, we shouldn't have to imagine them trying to do each other's jobs. They're good at their work and can be affirmed and approved for their respective roles. Their unique talents and skill sets help them do what they do well.

What might seem shocking is that each of these individuals works for the same organization. Using their unique skills and abilities, they all help the organization—in this case, their local church—pursue its mission and achieve its purpose. Erin serves by teaching kids in the church's school and equipping volunteers to serve alongside her. Marsha keeps the books and oversees the finances, Clayton keeps the facilities in tip-top shape, and Jacob leads the church's musicians and worship team. This diverse collection of talents and skills helps make the church (my church, to be more precise) operate effectively and pursue our shared purpose of glorifying God and making disciples. Without each of them, we couldn't do what we do nearly as well.

Having a diversely gifted team of leaders allows us to focus and lean into our strengths and abilities instead of doing things that fall outside our areas of expertise or competency. It gives us freedom from having to be the master of many different things and allows us to serve and work in the ways that best fit our passion, skills, talents, and gifts. The brilliant reality is that God has designed the church to be this kind of multicompetent, multigifted body that can serve and function well together, yet in distinct ways.

Before I start encouraging you to think about working at a church (I'll get there in a later chapter), I want to ask you whether you know where your gifting would best place you in laboring for the sake of the gospel. As I previously asked you to think about what you want to do with your life and career and how you can serve God's kingdom, I want to help you in this chapter to identify how your unique giftings might equip you for particular roles and enable you to meet specific needs around you. Dr. Seuss famously reminds us, "Today you are you! That is truer than true! There is no one alive who is you-er than you!"[1] If it's true that you're unique, fearfully and wonderfully made (Ps. 139:14), then it's also true that God has uniquely provided you with specific passions and gifts to deploy for his glory and the advance of the gospel. Do you know what those gifts are? That's an important first step in discerning your role in God's kingdom.

I want to encourage you to *make it your ambition to discern, develop, and deploy your unique giftings* to serve God and advance the gospel. Your uniqueness has a place in the body of Christ, and if you know these realities about yourself, you can find an effective place of service that will meet the needs of the moment in your local church and community. Your gifts are no accident, nor are the *when* and *where* of your life right now. God wants to use the details of your life and personality for his glory and the advancement of his kingdom.

You Have God-Given Gifts

You may be surprised to hear you're gifted. That might not even be a label you want applied to you. Yet if you're

1. Dr. Seuss, *Happy Birthday to You!* (Random House, 1959).

born again by God's Spirit (or saved), you're also gifted by the same Spirit who has made you alive. Jesus's life, death, and resurrection wasn't merely a work to rescue us from hell. His work also included a plan to impart his gifts to each member of his body (the church). God is giving and giving and giving. His salvation is all of grace, and everything else we have is grace and gift from him. Ephesians 2:8–9 teaches us, "For by grace you have been saved through faith. And this is not your own doing; it is the *gift* of God, not a result of works, so that no one may boast" (emphasis added).

With the gift of God's grace that saves us, he also showers us with the gift of his presence as the Holy Spirit indwells every believer (Rom. 8:11; 1 Cor. 12:12–13). From the love of the Father, the victory of Christ, and the presence of the Spirit, God brings down his gifts into our very lives. Paul describes this reality in Ephesians 4:7–8 when he says, "But grace was given to each one of us according to the measure of Christ's gift. Therefore it says, 'When he ascended on high he led a host of captives, and he gave gifts to men.'" These gifts that Paul continues to describe in Ephesians 4 are what we might today call "spiritual gifts." Each and every Christian is given gifts from God the Spirit. Or, as Paul says in 1 Corinthians 12:7, "To each is given the manifestation of the Spirit for the common good."

Being uniquely made, lovingly rescued, and intentionally gifted means you've been equipped by God for a distinct and specific purpose within the church. This is why it's important to discover what those gifts are.

Understand Spiritual Gifts

When discussing gifts and talents, we usually consider what strengths and abilities make us stand out from our peers. We might say someone who can slam-dunk a basketball is "gifted," as well as the person who can read something once, hold it in her memory, and word-for-word recount it at another time. But these talents or abilities aren't what the Bible talks about when it speaks of our gifting from the Holy Spirit.

Four specific passages in the New Testament give us a better understanding of spiritual gifts and how they're to be deployed.[2] Peter classifies the Spirit's gifts into the categories of speaking and serving (1 Pet. 4:11). Paul is more exhaustive in discussing the varieties of gifts, including messages of wisdom or knowledge, faith, healing, miracles, discernment, and speaking and interpreting tongues (1 Cor. 12:8–10). To the church in Rome, he talks about prophecy, serving, teaching, exhortation, generosity, leadership, and showing mercy (Rom. 12:6–8). The gifts he describes to the church in Ephesus seem more like the specific offices of apostles, prophets, evangelists, pastors, and teachers than types of gifts (Eph. 4:11). While these lists show a variety of spiritual gifts, their purpose is singular: to build up the body of Christ, the church (1 Cor. 14:12; Eph. 4:12).

With various gifts like these, it may not be easy to discern which gift or gifts you may have. Some have tried to put together spiritual gift assessments to help you discern by answering situational questions. While these

2. See Rom. 12:4–8; 1 Cor. 12:1–31; Eph. 4:4–16; 1 Pet. 4:10–11.

tests can provide a first impression of your gifting, they can also be misleading and manipulated to excuse Christians from emulating the Christlike behaviors encouraged in every believer. For example, if an assessment told me I don't have the gift of hospitality or mercy, I might tend to behave without showing hospitality or mercy, which are commanded of every Christian. Spiritual gifts aren't meant to define a boundary between ways you will and won't serve God's people.

So how do you discern what your gift might be? While the Spirit seems to gift people in ways that align with their personalities, interests, and passions, the gifts of the Spirit aren't personalities, talents, or desires. The gifts are particular empowerments of the Spirit to build the church (Eph. 4:12). The gifts are given as the Spirit discerns, desires, and imparts (1 Cor. 12:11). They aren't given to spotlight your life and abilities. There's a better question to ask: Where does your church need help? How can you leverage your time, energy, skills, and desires to serve, edify, and build up the church to help it flourish and advance the gospel?

You may find that your church leaders need people to serve by teaching children the Bible on Sunday mornings. You could offer to serve, meeting a need of the ministry, and discover you're gifted at teaching. Or you may learn there's a need in the church for visiting shut-ins and the sick. You could offer to meet the need of that ministry and discover along the way you have gifts of mercy. Perhaps the church lacks a ministry of prayer. Talk with your pastoral leadership about whether you could be part of starting regular prayer gatherings (discovering if you have gifts of leadership, administration, and faith).

You may find that, though you're willing to serve, you cannot fulfill the responsibilities or needs of a certain ministry. Don't be discouraged—you may not be gifted by the Spirit in the ways that particular role needs. It isn't wrong to ask the Spirit to supply those gifts to empower you to ministry in that area. But it could also mean there are different gifts the Spirit has given you for another role in the ministry of the church. Ask for another assignment.

The Holy Spirit is more inclined to supply gifts the local church needs rather than stockpiling similar gifts in one specific congregation. Discerning your gifts comes by asking where there are unmet ministry needs, asking the Holy Spirit to supply his gifts to fulfill and carry out that ministry, and seeking counsel and affirmation from your church leaders in acknowledging the gifts.

Develop and Deploy Your Gifts

Timothy was a young pastor. He'd received some of the world's best training and mentoring in ministry, and he was a promising young leader. By one means or another, he'd become the pastor of a local church in a large and notable city. But he felt the scope and weight of ministry responsibilities were overwhelming and beyond his abilities. Strong personalities within and outside the church demanded this and that from Timothy's ministry. Some were even eager to see him fail and wanted the church to close. He was fearful and floundering, thinking this responsibility was completely beyond him and worrying he'd wash out of ministry altogether.

That was until a letter from his mentor showed up at his door. Hearing that Timothy was struggling in ministry, the mentor sat down to write instructions and directions for this young pastor as he led his church. The mentor was especially concerned about the false teachers trying to exploit the inexperienced pastor. So he wrote to warn Timothy about them and to encourage him to persevere in his calling. As he began to conclude his letter, Paul (the mentor) spoke directly to Timothy about his gifting: "Until I come, devote yourself to the public reading of Scripture, to exhortation, to teaching. *Do not neglect the gift you have*" (1 Tim. 4:13–14, emphasis added).

In a follow-up letter written from the dark, damp, cold, underground confines of a Roman holding cell, Paul reminded Timothy, "Fan into flame the gift of God, which is in you" (2 Tim. 1:6). Simply put, Paul encouraged this young man in the faith and in his ministry service to develop and deploy his gifts for the purpose of the church. Timothy's congregation, the Ephesian church, needed clear and faithful teaching of the Scriptures. They needed a discerning and encouraging leader who could cut through the noise of the false ideologies and idolatries of the culture by exhorting the church to faithfulness in doctrine and love. Timothy had those gifts; they were identified and encouraged by both Paul and the church elders.

Timothy was being challenged to utilize and grow in the gifts God had given him for the sake of the church. He didn't need to sit them on the shelf and go off to do other things. Nor was he to think he was fully competent because he was given spiritual gifts and could coast in his responsibilities as someone "gifted." Paul commanded him, "Practice these things, immerse yourself in them, so that all may see your progress" (1 Tim. 4:15). The gifts that Timothy was given were meant to be used and matured.

The same is true of your gifting and ministry. I can't say it enough: God has gifted you with the ability to serve his people in a unique way. As you discover and are affirmed in your gifts, start working to excel in those areas of service. This may require further training and education. For instance, if your gifting is "as one who speaks" (1 Pet. 4:11), you should pursue training in interpreting the Bible, theological proficiency, and public speaking. Other gifting may not require formal education and training but can be matured and developed through mentoring, experience, and training. If you make it your ambition to discern and deploy your gifting in ministry, you'll ask, How can I grow in serving this way? What can I do to serve in the best way possible for the glory of God?

We'd find it strange if a physician quit reading current medical journals to keep up with advancing procedures that help treat and heal patients. Lawyers unfamiliar with current legal statutes and cases shouldn't be considered competent to handle their clients' issues. My point is to keep pressing forward in discerning, developing, and deploying the gifting God has given you.

For the Building of the Body

One major mistake we often make when thinking about the gifts of the Spirit revolves around how they're used.

This isn't a new problem; it's been an issue since the first expressions of the church after Pentecost. Our sinful desires, particularly our interest in getting into the spotlight, always seem to make a mess of the good gifts God gives. We often highlight the leaders who seem to have exceptional or extraordinary gifts to the exclusion of those who have more subtle, behind-the-scenes gifts. We affirm the upfront leaders and long to be noticed and celebrated for spectacular contributions to God's kingdom. Performing miracles is more desirable than practicing mercy.

If we focus only on the spiritual gifts that are seen and celebrated, we'll miss the overall purpose of the Spirit's gifts in our lives. But if we remember the root purpose of glorifying God and equipping the church, I believe we'll find a healthy and holy enjoyment of God's grace in our churches. The gifts aren't about *you*; they're about how God empowers and uses *you* to serve him and his people. The focus of our spiritual gifting must always be about how God is equipping you to advance the gospel and build up his people.

My friend and fellow pastor Rob talks about the church as "God's construction crew." He writes,

> Some of us survey the land. Others move the soil. Some of us dig holes for the placement of the cornerstone. Others pour the foundation. Some of us hammer and nail. And still others do the finish work. None are more important than any other. None

> deserve more honor than another. Nobody's role has more significance.[3]

The pastor who preaches, the person who manages the facilities, the woman who develops curricula and teaches kids, the accountant who keeps the books and manages the finances, the artist who prepares music and leads singing, and everyone else in the church has a place and purpose for their gifts. They're all necessary for building up and strengthening Christ's body. It isn't a matter of whether we have gifts; it's a matter of each person using his or her gifts and serving to see the whole grow and flourish.

This includes you. If you've placed your trust and faith in Jesus, then he has sent his Spirit to empower you to be part of God's construction crew. No Christian is exempt or excluded. We all have a place within the body and a calling to use the gifts the Spirit has supplied to build up his body. Because of this, it should be our lifelong ambition, no matter how great or small our gifts, to discern, develop, and deploy those gifts for the glory of Christ among his people. Make it your ambition!

Discussion Questions

1. What talents, gifts, or abilities do you possess that make you distinct from someone else?
2. Why are spiritual gifts given from God? How did you come to that answer?

3. Rob Bentz, *The Unfinished Church: God's Broken and Redeemed Work-in-Progress* (Crossway, 2014), 72.

3. What are your spiritual gifts? How do you know? If you don't know, how did this chapter encourage you to discern your spiritual gifting?
4. What are some ministries or ways of serving that can help you develop and use your gifts?
5. What would your life look like if you made it your ambition to discern, develop, and deploy your gifts and abilities?

4

Make It Your Ambition to Serve Others with Your Career

Up to this point, we've mainly talked about your relationship with God and how this relationship shapes your life. The chief ambitions of your life should be to know and love God, model the character of Christ, and discern and use the gifting of the Spirit. These ambitions are foundational and essential to every Christian. But I have an agenda in this book. I'm incrementally trying to persuade you to make the course of your life one that you may not have yet considered. When I was young, there was a storybook about a monster at the end of the book; similarly, there's a vocation at the end of this book. I hope that work will be something you're interested in and eager to pursue.

Let me dispel a myth as we get to talking about your work and career plans. I'm not going to suggest that Christian ministry is the only right and proper vocation for a child of God. God doesn't call or assign every Christian to be a missionary, pastor, ministry leader, or paid laborer in the church. The separation of "sacred" and "secular" vocations is often used to elevate those in paid ministry work above those in secular fields. Martin Luther argued that "there is no true, basic difference between laymen and priests, princes and bishops, or (as they say) between spiritual and secular, except that of office and work, and not that of status."[1] The architect is just as equal in his assignment and calling as the pastor. They just have different vocations. This means a vast array of work is valid and a "noble vocation." There's no greater spiritual esteem or value to being a cross-cultural missionary than to being a teacher in a local public school.

So let's talk about your future career and interests. Let's return to my first question: What do you want to do with your life? What career choices do you have? You may not be sure at this point. You may question why you'd even need to have a career. You may just go to college and do whatever strikes you as interesting and makes good money. Conversely, a host of questions and considerations could occupy your thoughts and leave you in a state of mental paralysis as you try to make a decision. How would you know what to do?

1. Martin Luther, "To the Christian Nobility of the German Nation Concerning the Improvement of the Christian Estate," in *The Roots of Reform*, ed. James M. Estes, Hans J. Hillerbrand, Kirsi I. Stjerna, and Timothy J. Wengert, vol. 1, *The Annotated Luther* (Fortress Press, 2015), 383.

Usually, in the Western world, this decision is left up to you. In reference to a career or job, most of us have been told, "You can do anything you want." That's part of the so-called American Dream. If you want to be a doctor, the doors can open for you to pursue that career. If you want to practice law, go for it! Suppose you want to be an accountant, teacher, plumber, police officer, computer scientist, astronaut, writer, or zoologist. There are ample opportunities for education and training to land careers in those fields. The door is often wide open for you to chase your dreams and be who you want to be.

In one sense, this is good. The abundant scope of opportunities for young adults today is welcome. I'm sure you're glad you aren't automatically forced into an occupation or role because that's what your father did or because the government dictates your station in life. But from another vantage point, this open-ended list of possibilities can be tremendously overwhelming. We want the agency and freedom to make our choices, but wouldn't it be helpful if someone narrowed down the options for us?

And one other challenge exists—the challenge of discerning *why* we should pursue a particular pathway. We live in a culture that elevates money above almost all else. You work your job to make the money you need and want. Financial independence and abundance are key goals. The predominant philosophy is to make as much money as possible to live a life of luxury. Yet we as Christ's followers should ask whether this is the primary goal of our work. Is working for 40-plus years to earn enough money to retire well and live "the good life" before we die all we should consider when picking a career? Is there is a greater purpose for our work?

New Perspectives on Purpose

A few years ago, I met a doctor who wasn't making much money. This wasn't because he was a lousy doctor or made poor decisions regarding his education, where he practiced medicine, or anything like that. In fact, he was very intentional about where he went to work. Kent Brantly was working in one of the poorest regions of the globe—West Africa. Not only was he practicing medicine among some of the poorest people in the world, but he was also working in a hot zone of the infectious viral disease Ebola. What began in spring 2014 turned into the largest Ebola outbreak in history since the virus was discovered in 1976.[2] Prior to the 2014 outbreak, the fatality rate was nearly 70 percent of those infected. By the time this outbreak subsided more than two years later, nearly 11,000 people had died of Ebola. Almost 30,000 were infected. Brantly was one of those infected by the virus as he treated patients at the ELWA Hospital outside of Monrovia, Liberia. After being transported to Emory University Hospital in Atlanta, Georgia, by a specialized medical evacuation air team, he was treated and survived the virus's lethal effects. When Brantly talks about why he chose to go to Liberia instead of enjoying a posh

2. "Ebola: West Africa, March 2014–2016," World Health Organization, accessed May 31, 2024, https://www.who.int/emergencies/situations/ebola-outbreak-2014-2016-West-Africa.

post-residency job at a well-established hospital within the safe confines of the United States, he concludes,

> My career choice was never about the pursuit of becoming a doctor. My goal was to find a way to serve people, and medicine was a career through which I could live a life of service. . . . Amber and I did not simply choose to go to Liberia. Instead, we decided to answer God's call on our lives to become medical missionaries.[3]

Brantly's expression of his work is through the lens of *vocation*, not merely a job. He sees his work as something far more significant than a means to make money and occupy his time before he retires and dies. This idea of vocation may be new to you. I'm not just talking about a career or a job you stay at for a long time. I live in southeast Michigan, where the auto industry has laid deep roots over many generations. I know men and women who've worked for one of the "Big Three" auto manufacturers for decades. They wouldn't, however, view their jobs as vocations. Many are unsatisfied and even discouraged by what they've spent the most significant portion of their lives doing. But they must pay the bills, provide for their children's education, and have something to do with their time. What could change their perspective from working a job to laboring in a vocation?

3. Kent Brantly and Amber Brantly with David Thomas, *Called for Life: How Loving Our Neighbor Led Us into the Heart of the Ebola Epidemic* (Waterbrook Press, 2015), 34, 45.

Though we seldom use the word "vocation," it's usually understood as a synonym for "career" or "job." It's the thing we spend 40-plus hours, 5 days a week doing. But the idea of vocation has a more profound and vital sense. Vocation comes from the Latin word *vocare*, which means "to call." It contains the idea of being called to something in order to serve someone.[4] I want to encourage you to see work as vocation. Doing so will give eternity-informed focus and purpose to your future work. Like Brantly, I want you to make your prospective job into a calling. I want you to *make it your ambition to serve others with your career*.

Paul spoke of this idea to the Corinthian believers when he told them, "Let each person lead the life that the Lord has assigned to him, and to which God has called him" (1 Cor. 7:17). A prominent idea stands out in this verse: God has *assigned* and *called* each of us to a position, role, or station in life. In his infinite wisdom and providential design for all things (including our individual lives), God has apportioned a specific set of responsibilities for us to carry out. We're called by God to "lead the life" that God has called us into. Furthermore, he's summoned us to fulfill that assignment or calling. God has said, here's what I have for you to do; do it! Tim Keller states,

> One of the hopes for our unraveling society is the recovery of the idea that all human work is not merely a job but a *calling*. . . . A job is a vocation only if

4. Timothy Keller and Katherine Leary Alsdorf, *Every Good Endeavor: Connecting Your Work to God's Work* (Dutton, 2012), 19.

> someone else calls you to do it and you do it for them rather than for yourself. And so our work can be a calling only if it is reimagined as a mission of service to something beyond merely our own interests.[5]

Not only does vocation carry the sense of being appointed or called by someone to do something, but it assigns a larger purpose to what we do. Our vocations *serve* someone else. Ultimately, that service is unto the Lord, but it's also a service to humanity.

How would your idea of your future and your career change if you looked at your occupation through the lens of vocation? What has God assigned you to do, and how are you pursuing that calling? How are you serving God and your fellow human beings in this calling from the Lord?

I realize that when I tell you that God has an assignment he calls each of us to do, it presents a broader scope of concerns. For instance, you may be worried about trying to find that *exact* assignment God has called you to. You may fear that if you mistakenly pursue the wrong thing, you won't be fulfilled, or God may be disappointed in you. You may be concerned you'll be called and assigned by God to do something you have no interest in, forcing you into a life of misery, difficulty, and discouragement. I had a friend in college who was convinced that God would make her live in India, the *last* place she ever wanted to go. Such concerns may have a strand of validity, especially if we already have career desires or

5. Keller and Alsdorf, *Every Good Endeavor*, 19.

ambitions of our own. How do we know if our career aspirations are the same things as God's assignments?

My Ambitions Versus God's Assignment

Maybe you feel something of a struggle here. You have a career in mind, but you're torn because you want to please the Lord and live under the assignment he's given you (and you assume the two are at odds). I call this the Hermey Conundrum. Hermey is the elf from the 1964 animated TV special *Rudolph the Red-Nosed Reindeer*. Being an elf meant he was a toymaker. "You're an elf, and elves make toys!" his boss yells at him.[6] But Hermey didn't like making toys (and he wasn't very good at it). Instead, Hermey wanted to be a dentist. The world of dentistry fascinated him. He was torn between a personal ambition and what seemed like a superimposed assignment he had no choice in. Is the Hermey Conundrum a reality that God might box you into?

I can assure you that God isn't the angry supervisor elf shaming us for our desires when we should be fulfilling some mysterious alternate obligation. He hasn't manufactured some secret duty, unknown to us, that cuts against what we'd rather pursue. Yet there is a secret in how our ambitions and God's assignments align.

Psalm 139 reflects on God's creation of and intimate knowledge of us. David confesses, "Lord, you have searched me and known me. You know when I sit down and when I stand up; you understand my thoughts from

6. *Rudolph the Red-Nosed Reindeer*, directed by Larry Roemer, aired December 6, 1964, on NBC.

far away" (Ps. 139:1–2, CSB). The first 12 verses of the psalm proclaim the depth and totality of God's knowledge of us. From our thoughts and words to our physical location, God isn't unaware or ignorant of who we are. And that's good news for us. God isn't surprised one bit by your desires and aspirations for your life. He's not overwhelmed in astonishment that you might want to be a dentist instead of a toymaker. Here's why, and this is the secret answer to the tension between our assignments and aspirations: *God made us with those aspirations and, as long as we pursue them with Christlike character, he wants us to chase them down!*

David essentially says, "God, you know me perfectly, deeply, and thoroughly." There's nothing hidden or unknown about us that catches God off guard. That's all because God formed and fashioned us with these aspirations and desires. David goes on to say,

> For it was *you* who created my inward parts;
> you knit me together in my mother's womb.
> I will praise you
> because I have been remarkably and wondrously *made*. (vv. 13–14, CSB)

David isn't only talking about the formation of our physical bodies and internal organs. He's capturing the reality that God is the One who has formed and fashioned *everything* about us. He continues to describe God's intricate fashioning of us: "Your eyes saw me when I was formless; all my days were written in your book and planned before a single one of them began" (v. 16, CSB). *You* were seen and known by God completely before you spent five minutes out of the womb. He has ordained your days in such a way that your God-given desires and pursuits are hardwired into them. What this means for those of us stuck in the Hermey Conundrum is that your personal preferences and pursuits are most likely the very things that God has assigned and ordained for you to do anyway. I'd tell Hermey he should pursue dentistry. He's probably called to it. God placed that desire and interest in his heart before he was ever born, and it's authentically Hermey's dream as much as it is God's vocational call to him. Quit the toy factory and enroll in dental school![7]

This reality that God has intentionally formed us with unique desires and interests—interests that are most likely the assignments he has appointed for us—should give us great freedom to shake off the fear of making a mistake or running after what we weren't designed or duty-bound to do. What we must be aware of is making sure our desires and ambitions align with God's overall framework for our lives. That vocational framework is simply this: "Love the Lord your God with all your heart and with all your soul and with all your strength and with all your mind, and your neighbor as yourself" (Luke 10:27). Under this framework, you have the freedom and open field to pursue any vocational ambition that excites and motivates you. If your career ambitions are primarily oriented around loving God, you can be sure they're aligned with God's assignment for you. You

7. I also want to recognize that your career or vocation might not stay the same over the course of your life. Different realities and seasons in life may bring about changes to your career and calling that only that season can determine. Continue to be prayerful about your desires and impulses regarding God's calling.

need not fear Hermey's Conundrum. Yet the framework of your life isn't only about your relationship with God. It has a horizontal (one-another) reality that directs the second component of a vocation: loving your neighbor as yourself.

Aim to Serve

How does your desired career path function to serve God and benefit humanity? What contribution to the kingdom of God and society does your career trajectory lend itself toward?

What I'm asking you to consider here is the end or goal of your work. Many can say they sensed a calling to one profession or another and became successful, yet the end pursuit of that professional life was all about themselves. It's all too possible to take up a noble profession and work demanding hours only for personal material profit and professional acclaim. Money can easily become the god you serve, work, and live for. The sad reality the Preacher of Ecclesiastes noted is that you can live a long life, be successful in all you do, acquire great wealth, and at the end of the day, still die and "leave it to the man who will come after [you], and who knows whether he will be wise or a fool?" (Eccl. 2:18–19). When you die, you won't take one cent with you. What will last and be of value is the lives of others you've served and blessed.

In some cases, it's easy to determine whether an occupation is only about serving yourself and making money versus being a vocation that serves others *and* provides an income for you to live on. In most cases, however, there's a mixture of factors at play. This is why the vocational perspective is needed. Kent Brantly is still working in the medical field. He survived the Ebola virus and even returned to minister and serve as a doctor in places where poverty, famine, and war have torn everything apart. He has also worked in hospitals and medical practices in the United States and made a good income. His perspective on vocation has guided him in making decisions in various contexts and opportunities. By viewing his work as a calling to serve others, he can take positions in hot zones and also work in a metropolitan area in a well-appointed American hospital. He's not guided by the ambition to serve money. He's guided by the ambition to serve God and help those suffering from affliction and illness.

Gospel-Informed View of Work

We should call this a gospel-informed view of work. If one of our life ambitions is to model Christ's character, shouldn't we have the same perspective on our work and occupations as Jesus did? He saw his work as a vocational calling. He was assigned and called by his Father to be the only mediator between God and humanity. He "gave himself as a ransom for all" (1 Tim. 2:6), serving and suffering for humanity's sake. Jesus's ministry was a vocational calling that served God and humanity.

Our assignments are different. We can't atone for humanity's sin and stand as the only mediator. But we share in Jesus's vocation by living in the assignment and calling God has given us, seeking to serve and benefit our neighbors through our labor and industry.

Let me encourage you to take your potential future career and assess its vocational nature. How will it benefit others? How will it serve God? What influence will your career have for God's glory? Let me add one last consideration to your mind: Have you given any thought to a vocation in Christian ministry? Could you be called and assigned to serve in medical missions? Maybe God has gifted you to use your talents and skills by working for a local church. Perhaps you're gifted and skilled in administration and leadership. Instead of being a corporate middle manager, would you consider serving a Christian institution such as a seminary, church, or campus ministry? Maybe instead of taking that communication degree into a corporate marketing setting, you can use it to help Christian ministries get the gospel message out through social media marketing and management.

Ultimately, whether you end up in Christian ministry or not, if you make it your ambition to serve God and others vocationally, you'll fulfill his design for you in the work he has given you. You'll spend the hours and strength of your life outliving yourself, living for the glory of God and the good of others. A life of vocational perspective, being called and assigned by God to serve him and others, is a life full of kingdom influence. Make it your ambition to serve others vocationally.

Discussion Questions

1. What career or job interests do you have or are you pursuing? What made you interested in those jobs?
2. How is the concept of *vocation* different than just an occupation or career?

3. Have you ever considered what God's vocational assignment or calling is for your life? Why or why not?
4. How does the gospel message inform or shape your view of a career, job, and vocation?
5. What would your life look like if you made it your ambition to serve others with your career?

5

Make It Your Ambition to Share the Gospel

If you had water, would you give it to a person dying of thirst? If you were a trauma surgeon, would you operate on a person dying of a fatal wound? If you were a firefighter, would you go in and rescue the child caught in the burning building? If you were a skilled swimmer and lifeguard, would you jump into the pool to save the drowning child? Apart from the nuances that may or may not condition each of these scenarios, I'd like to believe you'd be eager to help and assist those suffering in some way or another. Most likely, you'd be quick to serve and give a hand to do what you could to keep another person in peril alive. Unless, perhaps, you were climbing Mount Everest.

There's a region above 26,000 feet on the Everest climb known as the Death Zone. Up at that elevation, your body cannot get enough oxygen to operate correctly.

At this altitude, breathing is laboriously difficult. Most climbers require the use of supplemental oxygen tanks to enable them to make the push to the summit. The altitude isn't the only barrier to reaching the top. The climb demands a significant level of physical fitness and mountaineering capabilities. If you go for the summit from the south side of the mountain in Nepal, you have to make multiple crossings over a section of glacier known as the Khumbu Icefall. It's a perilous maze of crevices, moving ice, and treacherous steps that require a group of mountaineers known as Icefall Doctors to place fixed ropes and ladders through to assist their clients in getting up it. If you come at the summit from the north on the Tibetan Plateau, you must ascend steep, sheer walls of rock at the highest altitudes. Making the summit of Everest is no sure thing.

Apart from the climb's physical toll, you also commit to a substantial financial investment. A good guide company typically hires Sherpa porters to guide the climb, prepare meals, and help haul the gear so you have the best shot at standing on the top. This costs anywhere from $70,000 to $85,000. Plus, it involves months and months of training, travel, and actual climbing. The personal, physical, and financial investment required to reach the top is astronomical.

These factors explain why, if you were climbing Everest, you might be less inclined to help someone in trouble. You would've worked too hard, paid too much, and given up too much to make it to the highest point on the planet.

This scenario plays out every year. Mark Synnott, in his book *The Third Pole*, talks about the dead bodies lying on the summit routes of Everest, frozen in place. It's too expensive, difficult, and dangerous to retrieve their bodies for burial elsewhere. When climbers come across someone in trouble from hypoxia or overexertion, they have to make a choice. To assist someone in distress is to give up your attempt to reach the top. Most pass by, say a prayer, and hope for the best. Synnott tells of one climber in recent years who was in distress and was ignored by climbers going up and down. No one helped him, and he perished not far from the summit.[1]

When you evaluate the motives of why an able person would or wouldn't save someone in distress on Mount Everest, one answer becomes clear: most of us would help someone in trouble if it didn't also imperil us. The ethical algorithms of our hearts would be quick to help someone in need if it didn't come at the cost of our own lives. This philosophy would cause us to retreat into self-preservation mode if it meant we'd end up losing our lives or missing out on our goals.

Here's my question: Why do we often treat the spiritual condition of those around us as if we're climbing Mount Everest and would be putting ourselves in danger if we helped them? Why don't we rather see their danger and need, and then reach out to help? Why—when we consider our friends, roommates, fellow students, even coworkers—do we balk at sharing the only hope of life instead of caring for them by sharing the gospel?

I want to encourage you and your generation to see the desperate need of those around you—the spiritual

1. Mark Synnott, *The Third Pole: Mystery, Obsession, and Death on Mount Everest* (Dutton, 2022), 314ff.

peril of sinners headed to an eternity of judgment—and having embraced the gospel by faith, I hope you'll be eager and active to share it with those who need Christ. I want to challenge you to *make it your ambition to share the gospel.*

The Need Is Urgent

Before discussing the practical how-tos and what-to-dos in sharing the gospel, I want to elaborate on why it's needed. Perhaps we don't feel deeply or act directly in sharing our faith because we don't fully absorb the reality of the plight and spiritual danger so many live under. Many times, we picture sharing the gospel as being a loud and aggressive person on a street corner with a big "Jesus Hates You" sign and a megaphone shouting down God's wrath on wicked people. We don't want to offend or anger people by telling them they sit under God's judgment for their sin and are headed to hell if they don't believe in Jesus. Evangelism implies some degree of judgment about another person's condition, and we don't want to be judgy people.

Suppose we could set aside for a moment our preconceived notions of evangelism (the street preacher or judgmental legalist) and discuss *why* we need to share the gospel. If we can, we'll be able to get clarity on why evangelism should be an ambition in our lives. Let me offer two reasons why sharing the gospel is needed.

1. Sharing the Gospel Tells the Truth and Makes Much of God

The biggest lie ever told in the history of the world was the lie that God isn't who he claims to be. Satan told this lie to our first parents, Adam and Eve, in the garden when he cast doubt into Eve's mind regarding God's character. He brazenly lied and told the couple that God wasn't interested in their ultimate well-being and happiness. According to the lie, God was withholding true good from them and wasn't who he claimed to be. Sadly, both our first parents and all of humanity bought the lie.

The lie is perpetuated today in various forms and fashions. We're told that God isn't as gracious and merciful as the Bible says, so we have to earn his affection by our moral and religious behavior. Or we're told that God isn't as just and righteous as he professes to be, so there are no real consequences for us if we go against what he says. The lie has been exaggerated to the degree that many wonder if there really is a God at all.

When we share the gospel message, we tell the truth about God. We declare that God is both gracious and just. He loves to save sinners from spiritual death and their sin, but he'll also judge unrepentant sinners. This is the very truth God shares as he reveals his glory to Moses in Exodus 33 and 34. Moses wants to know and see God clearly, so he requests to see God's glory. God, however, knows no person can fully perceive the glory of the Lord and live. Still, God invites Moses to come up to the mountain the next day, where God will hide him "in a cleft of the rock" (33:22), and then, once God has passed by, Moses will be allowed to see him from the back. What we read next isn't a description of Moses seeing God; instead, we hear what God says about himself before Moses.

> The Lord passed before him and proclaimed, "The Lord, the Lord, a God merciful and gracious, slow to anger, and abounding in steadfast love and faithfulness, keeping steadfast love for thousands, forgiving iniquity and transgression and sin, but who will by no means clear the guilty, visiting the iniquity of the fathers on the children and the children's children, to the third and the fourth generation." (34:6–7)

God declared the truth of who he is to Moses, and it's the truth that God is fully loving, intensely compassionate and patient, full of grace and kindness. But it's also true that God will "by no means clear the guilty." When we share the gospel, we illuminate the truth, and in doing so, we make much of God. Sharing the gospel's good news means we tell the truth about God and, therefore, elevate him above all rival gods or saviors.

2. People Believe in Christ Because They've Heard the Gospel

Maybe you've heard the expression "Preach the gospel at all times, and when necessary, use words." The idea isn't totally wrong, yet it's incomplete. Yes, our friends and neighbors must see by how we live that the gospel is true and we've been transformed. Jesus told his disciples that the new way of life included loving each other: "Just as I have loved you, you also are to love one another"

(John 13:34). He goes on to say, "By this all people will know that you are my disciples, if you have love for one another" (v. 35). Francis Schaeffer, one of the most helpful thinkers and theologians of the 20th century, remarked, "Upon His authority He gives the world the right to judge whether you and I are born-again Christians on the basis of our observable love toward all Christians."[2] Preaching the gospel does require living in step with the gospel. The world should be able to observe that we have transformed lives.

Yet you can't preach the gospel without words. Verbally sharing the good news is necessary. Paul knew this to be true when he reflected in Romans 10 about what's needed for people to be saved from Satan, sin, and death. His line of argument is tight. First, the promise is that "everyone who calls on the name of the Lord will be saved" (Rom. 10:13). But Paul asks, "How, then, can they call on the one they have not believed in?" (v. 14, NIV). A person has to be able to believe in Christ if she's going to call on Christ to save her. In saying that, Paul adds another important layer: a person has to *hear* about Christ to believe in Christ. Paul's next two rhetorical questions make this need obvious: "And how can they believe in the one of whom they have not heard? And how can they hear without someone preaching to them?" (v. 14, NIV). Don't get stumped by the word "preaching." Here it just means someone telling or proclaiming Christ to another person. Paul makes his point by saying, "Faith comes from hearing, and hearing through the word of Christ"

2. Francis A. Schaeffer, *The Complete Works of Francis A. Schaeffer: A Christian Worldview*, vol. 4 (Crossway, 1982), 187.

(v. 17). As a result, *for someone to believe in Christ and call on him as Lord and Savior, he needs to have someone go to him and speak the gospel message to him*.

The exhortation then should really be this: "Preach the gospel at all times, and since it's necessary, use words." Your non-Christian friends, family members, and neighbors will not believe the message of Christ without hearing it. Yes, they need to see the gospel message's authenticity lived out, but they must also hear the message itself.

If we agree that sharing the gospel is necessary because doing so tells the truth about God and exalts him, and it's the only means by which people can turn and believe in Jesus, wouldn't that make sharing the gospel a critical ambition for our lives? Shouldn't we want to love God and our neighbors as best as possible by explaining what he has done for us in Christ? It's one of the most loving things we can do.

Ambassadors, Not Sales Professionals

Have you ever shared the gospel message of Jesus's perfect life, substitutionary death, and glorious resurrection as a person's only hope and salvation? If so, how did it go? You might think of sharing the gospel message as a win-or-lose scenario. Either the person you share with comes to faith in Christ, or she says "No thanks" and pushes away your attempts to win her to Jesus. This all-or-nothing perspective can make evangelism daunting. We're worried about doing it wrong or making a friendship or working relationship awkward. If you imagine that sharing your faith means being a sales and marketing professional, you'll probably feel uncomfortable doing it.

First-century Christians and church leaders had a different perspective on their role in sharing the good news of Christ. They didn't see themselves as sales professionals or social media influencers trying to push a product. They envisioned themselves as ambassadors representing a gracious and powerful King and his kingdom. They saw sharing the faith as inviting rebellious, lost, and hurting people to become citizens of a peaceable, loving, and whole kingdom of grace. Paul likened himself to an ambassador with a ministry of reconciliation:

> That is, in Christ God was reconciling the world to himself, not counting their trespasses against them, and entrusting to us the message of reconciliation. Therefore, we are ambassadors for Christ, God making his appeal through us. We implore you on behalf of Christ, be reconciled to God. (2 Cor. 5:19–20)

Brought down to its most basic reality, evangelism is working for relational reconciliation between God and humanity. Yes, it involves imploring and appealing to the hearts and minds of people who are relationally estranged from God, but evangelism isn't selling heaven or your best life now. You might be asking yourself what it means, then, to be an effective witness. Growing as an ambassador of Christ to your lost friends, neighbors, and coworkers will take development of your skills. You need to grow in two key competencies to be effective.

1. Know the Gospel

To be a capable ambassador, you must understand and embrace the gospel yourself. It has to be real for your life. You cannot commend, implore, or appeal to someone else to reconcile with God if you haven't reconciled with him yourself. Sure, you can say the right words and declare truths, but if you've yet to embrace and be transformed by the good news of Christ, you won't find evangelism a compelling ambition for your life.

Knowing the gospel also means understanding the concrete details and facts of the gospel message. If you're going to be an ambassador and represent the message of Christ and his kingdom, you should be familiar with the message. How is reconciliation with God possible? What must someone know, believe, and do to be reconciled to God?

Biblical passages such as John 3:16, 1 Corinthians 15:1–8, and 1 Timothy 1:15 and 2:5, as well as an outline called The Romans Road,[3] provide solid texts for knowing and embracing the gospel. There are also helpful resources such as Greg Gilbert's *What Is the Gospel?* and Matt Chandler and Jared Wilson's *The Explicit Gospel*, which give clear and reproducible explanations of the gospel message. The point is that to be effective, you must know this message clearly and have personally experienced redemption in Christ.

3. Romans 1:16–17; 3:23; 5:8; 6:23; and 10:9–10 are signposts on this simple path of Scriptures that lay out a gospel invitation.

2. Speak the Gospel

If you know and have embraced the gospel's dynamic truth in your life, then being effective as an ambassador also entails being able to speak or share the gospel with someone else. Here's where you open your mouth and talk about Jesus. It's a necessary Christian skill to be able to talk someone through the story of redemption and explain the high points of (1) God as our holy and good Creator, (2) humanity as fallen rebels, (3) God as Redeemer, (4) Christ as our sacrificial substitute, and (5) the necessity of our response.[4] You have to be able to give someone a whole picture of his need and God's solution so he can understand and respond.

Growing in effectiveness also means developing the skills of speaking personally and publicly. You may not ever be called to share the gospel from a stage or platform in a formal way, but you should be able to speak about it to even a small group of people. If you want to be able to do this well, taking classes in public speaking, practicing sharing the gospel with a group of Christian friends, or just jumping in and sharing the gospel with non-Christians will provide an immediate crash course in how to communicate the truth of God's grace. Look for ways to get practice sharing the gospel verbally and publicly.

One way to do this is to become a curious person with those you're close to who don't know Christ. By "curious," I mean you should ask questions about what

4. These five "movements," as I call them, are an essential outline of the gospel message.

they think or believe about God; about the brokenness of the world; about their needs, their anxieties, and what affects their daily lives. Ask open-ended questions so you can hear their perspectives. Then, if the opportunity presents itself, share the gospel truth you carry. Ask them if they'd like to know more about what you believe and ask the Holy Spirit to lead you in sharing with them.

Ambition for Life

If you see the desperate need of those around you for the gospel and lean into being an ambassador of reconciliation on Christ's behalf, you'll find sharing the gospel is part and parcel of your life. You'll faithfully commend God and his grace to the lost and dying. Instead of ignoring or overlooking those in need in your pursuit of whatever summit you're climbing, you'll stop and offer aid to a whole planet that lives in a spiritual Death Zone. I don't know of any more significant or higher ambition a person can have than to share the gospel.

Do you have this ambition in your life? Maybe by making you aware of the great need and our responsibility as Christians, I've planted this calling in your heart. Perhaps it was already there, and this chapter has been the rocket fuel you needed to propel you forward. Whatever the case, if this ambition is in your heart, I want to drop a further idea in your head that I'll develop later.

Many Christians I know who are zealous, faithful, and competent in sharing their faith have ventured into serving in vocational Christian ministry. Many work vocationally as cross-cultural missionaries, campus ministry staff, or in church contexts as pastors, ministers, or staff. It's not a complete parallel that you *must* go into vocational ministry if you have this ambition. Still, if you're eager, engaged, and effective in proclaiming and sharing the gospel, you could be called to vocational ministry.

So far, the prior ambitions I've called you to embrace—knowing and loving God, modeling Christ's character, developing your gifts and talents, and serving others with your work and vocation—have been ambitions every Christian should embody. This is the same for the ambition to share the gospel. However, a deeper passion and ability to share the gospel effectively indicates a competency not every Christian possesses. If you do have that desire, let me drop the hint (for now) that you should give thought to pursuing a vocation in Christian ministry.

When Jesus saw the spiritual plight of the multitudes in the Death Zone, "he had compassion on them, because they were harassed and helpless, like sheep without a shepherd" (Matt. 9:36, NIV). He helped his disciples to see that the harvest was big and ready. Yet he said, "The laborers are few; therefore pray earnestly to the Lord of the harvest to send out laborers into his harvest" (vv. 37–38). You're one of those laborers God is sending into his harvest. Make it your ambition to share the gospel with everyone you can.

Discussion Questions

1. What keeps us from sharing the gospel with the non-Christians in our lives?

2. Which reason for sharing the gospel resonated with you? What other reasons might there be for sharing the gospel?
3. How does having the perspective of an ambassador (rather than a salesperson) help encourage you to share the gospel?
4. What skills or competencies do you need to grow in to become more able in sharing the gospel?
5. What would your life look like if you made it your ambition to share the gospel with everyone you can?

6

Make It Your Ambition to Endure Hardship

Do you know what it cost to put a man on the moon? Financially, the figure is around $28 billion.[1] When you start calculating beyond money, you see that from a time and labor perspective, the cost was exponentially higher. Then you think about the loss of life that happened as the NASA space program developed, and the cost becomes incalculable. And yet, landing Neil Armstrong and Buzz Aldrin on the moon in July 1969 was one of humanity's greatest achievements.

Start working out the price paid to bring about the end of the Holocaust and the defeat of Nazi Germany. Both financially and physically, the cost is beyond

1. William Harwood, "Apollo 11: How Much Did It Cost to Land Astronauts on the Moon?" CBS News, July 16, 2019, https://www.cbsnews.com/news/apollo-11-moon-landing-how-much-did-it-cost/.

measure. Yet Allied nations joining together to defeat Hitler and end the extermination of the Jewish people during World War II was a triumph of international cooperation and the defeat of tyranny. It couldn't have happened apart from great sacrifice and perseverance.

It took Michelangelo four years to produce the greatest artistic masterpiece of the Renaissance: the ceiling of Rome's Sistine Chapel. Giving four years of your life to stand on a high scaffolding and paint what some would call the greatest painting ever is a commitment and investment. It didn't happen without sweat, tears, sacrifice, and a significant cost to Michelangelo.

What did it cost for Michael Phelps, the most awarded Olympic athlete of all time, to win 28 medals in swimming, all but 5 of them gold medals? What was the investment and dedication required for Serena Williams to win 23 tennis Grand Slam singles titles across her career? One more, since I like mountaineering: What did it cost Tenzing Norgay and Edmund Hillary to summit Mount Everest for the first time? Was each of these feats worth it?

When you put together a list of the greatest human achievements, you begin to see a shared reality. None of these triumphs came easily. Not one glorious ambition was fulfilled on the path of ease or least resistance. In contrast, each great and worthy pursuit has come at great cost to those who fought for a righteous cause, pushed the limits of exploration, committed to sharing their talents, or aimed to break a record.

We're getting down to the crux of this book, and I want to help you navigate carefully through the final two ambitions I'll set before you. So far, I've challenged you to set your aspirations and ambitions to lofty and glorious things. Ambitions like living to know and love God, modeling Christ's character, and taking up a vocation of service for God's glory are no small pursuits. Dedicating your life to these great and noble undertakings is a worthy endeavor. But how are you going to get there? What will it take for you to succeed in these or any other noble ambition you pursue?

I understand you may not have ambitions as extreme as being the first human on Mars. You may not aspire to own all the world records in pickleball or end a great injustice in society. Your goals may be more modest and down-to-earth like wanting to serve your community effectively, or own a business, or make a difference in someone's life. No matter what form your ambition takes, it should always be pursued as an extension of your desire to walk faithfully as a follower of Christ and serve his kingdom. As you move forward with that mindset, it should come as no surprise that a disciple's life will involve both effort and adversity. Whatever you do as a follower of Jesus, and wherever you go from this point on, I must urge you to *make it your ambition to endure hardship*. Work to build fortitude, resilience, and a persevering heart so that in whatever Christ calls you to, you'll be faithful and full of integrity in the end.

The Road Less Traveled

Perhaps you've encountered Robert Frost's most famous poem, "The Road Not Taken." He quips, "Two roads diverged in a yellow wood, / And sorry I could not travel both . . ." As the poem wanders through Frost's meditation on the two paths he encountered, he comes to a conclusion about the route he did choose: "Two roads diverged in a wood, and I—/ I took the one less traveled by, / And that has made all the difference."[2] Some have commented that the conclusion of Frost's idea is that a person should "seize the day" and look for the harder and more challenging paths to wander down in life. Taking the road less traveled can lead to better results and distinguish a person from those inclined to merely go along with the crowd or take the highways of life instead of the single-track trails that lead to mountain summits.

Regardless of how you interpret the poem's meaning, the idea of a road less traveled is simultaneously romantic and repulsive. We're creatures of habit, folks who enjoy the paths of least resistance. Doing hard things in our culture is, well, *hard*. Yet the people who do the hard things or expend great effort receive the great rewards their exertion affords them. We all see the results they attain of wealth, fame, and status (and perhaps desire them ourselves), but achieving those results is rarely the product of just being born.

My point in drawing attention to the road less traveled is to highlight that *any* worthwhile ambitions will cost something. It'll take effort to pursue them, especially the ambitions I've already laid out in this book. The apostle Paul knew this intimately. His life devoted for the glory of God, the advance of the gospel, and the hope of the kingdom to come was driven by the passionate

2. Robert Frost, "The Road Not Taken," Poetry Foundation, accessed June 28, 2024, https://www.poetryfoundation.org/poems/44272/the-road-not-taken.

pursuit of those goals. But they didn't come to reality by passive, effortless aspiration.

Paul articulated one of his greatest ambitions in this way: "My goal is to know [Christ] and the power of his resurrection and the fellowship of his sufferings, being conformed to his death, assuming that I will somehow reach the resurrection from among the dead" (Phil. 3:10–11, CSB). His desire and pursuit in life was no longer to have his religious performance be what identified or defined him. Instead, Paul's great ambition was to know and be like Christ. This aim is an Everest-level goal for life, and Paul knew it. It'll take a lot of work to attain or reach. To summit or achieve any great ambition, one must take the road less traveled—the road of enduring hardship.

The Right Stuff

How does someone build fortitude and resilience? If the ability to realize any of these ambitions for life comes down to being able to press on and press through the obstacles that stand in the way, how does someone get to where she can endure the difficulties thrown at her? How can Christians "make it" when they aspire to know and love God or share the gospel? To grow in endurance and the ability to suffer hardship, four elements must be present: perspective, priorities, perspiration, and power.

1. Perspective

Being able to endure hardship requires a new perspective about yourself, your circumstances, and your ambitions.

Succeeding in your pursuits isn't merely a result of those achievements being handed to you. We need the mentality of a committed soldier.

When Paul lays down his charge to Timothy to be faithful in ministry and to "entrust [the gospel] to faithful men, who will be able to teach others also" (2 Tim. 2:2), he doesn't just give Timothy that charge without helping shape his perspective. In the next statement, he tells Timothy to "share in suffering as a good soldier of Christ Jesus" (v. 3). To accomplish his aim of laboring for the gospel's sake and passing it on to able and trained men, he needs to endure and press through hardship. But don't miss the perspective he supplies to Timothy: "like a good soldier." Paul's direction to Timothy here makes me think of Steve Rogers (or Captain America) saying to the bullies in his neighborhood or the great supervillain he's taking a beating from, "I can do this all day."[3] It's a soldier's mentality.

In laying out a perspective for Timothy of endurance in the ministry, Paul supplies three metaphors: a soldier, an athlete, and a farmer (vv. 4–6). Each of these vocations requires a perspective and mentality of endurance. Those pursuing them have to push through the difficulties, trials, and obstacles that would keep them from being successful and obtaining their goals. If they're going to be successful, they must go into their pursuits with the mentality that what they're doing will be difficult and costly. There'll be opposition, hard days, sleepless nights, difficult labor, and potentially even physical danger.

3. *Captain America: The First Avenger*, directed by Joe Johnston (Marvel Studios, 2011).

Taking on a soldier's perspective doesn't mean picking fights and going to battle with everyone you meet. It means understanding that pursuing anything worthwhile for God's kingdom will be difficult, and we should accept the challenge.

Charles Simeon was the son of a wealthy man.[4] His father wanted him to have the best and live a relatively easy and comfortable life. Charles was well educated, and at 19 he enrolled at Cambridge University. Although Charles wasn't a Christian, students were required to attend Christian worship services and Bible classes. During Easter of his first year, Charles heard the gospel, and God opened his heart to believe. His life was transformed, and he began pursuing biblical studies and theology classes. Upon graduation, he was given a teaching fellowship at the university, and his father helped influence the local bishop to appoint Charles the pastor of a renowned church in Cambridge, Trinity Church. Life was going well for Charles.

But the congregation of Trinity didn't want Charles to be their pastor. They liked the assistant pastor and his lectures better. Charles held the theological convictions that the Bible is God's inspired Word, that Christ is the only Savior, and that salvation comes by God's grace alone through faith alone in Christ alone. The assistant pastor held none of those convictions, and the church wanted a pastor who'd "tickle their ears" (see 2 Tim. 4:3). When Charles would preach, they didn't attend services; when

4. To learn more about Charles Simeon, see Handley Carr Glyn Moule, *Charles Simeon: Biography of the Great Anglican Preacher and Evangelical Christian* (IVP, 1948).

they did show up, they prevented him from preaching. The church had a tradition of holding a second service on Sunday afternoons, and the congregation was given the privilege of choosing who they wanted to teach at that service. For seven years, it was never Charles. The congregation would avoid the first service and come to the second service, where the assistant pastor would teach. When Charles tried to start a third service, the congregation changed the locks and kept him from entering the building. Given this kind of hardship, Charles might have given up.

He didn't. Instead, he persevered, continued to show up, preached to whoever would listen, and sought to be faithful. He didn't abandon his calling, his church, or his Lord. After 49 years of ministry at Trinity, and the attitude change in the congregation due to Charles's faithfulness and pastoral care, one of his friends asked how he made it through all the hardship and difficulty. He replied, "My dear brother, we must not mind a little suffering for Christ's sake. . . . Let us rejoice in the remembrance that our holy Head has surmounted all His suffering and triumphed over death. Let us follow Him patiently; we shall soon be partakers of His victory."[5] Charles had the perspective of a faithful, dutiful soldier.

5. H. C. G. Moule, *Charles Simeon* (IVP, 1948), 155f, quoted in John Piper, "Brothers, We Must Not Mind a Little Suffering: Meditations on the Life of Charles Simeon," from 1989 Bethlehem Conference for Pastors, April 15, 1989, https://www.desiringgod.org/messages/brothers-we-must-not-mind-a-little-suffering.

2. Priorities

Paul not only commended to Timothy a soldier's perspective but also challenged him to embody a soldier's priorities. After encouraging Timothy to "share in suffering," Paul reminded him how a soldier relates to his commanding officers and the rest of the world. He told Timothy, "No soldier gets entangled in civilian pursuits, since his aim is to please the one who enlisted him" (2 Tim. 2:4). The soldier focuses on fulfilling orders and pleasing the commanding officer. He can't do whatever he'd like or please himself. Good soldiers have focus; they have priorities and want to achieve victory. As a result, they don't become wrapped up in the same sorts of things a civilian would.

Paul makes the point that to endure suffering and persevere through difficulty, our priorities must be straight. We can't chase every dream, whim, desire, or fancy that floats into our heads. There must be a "long obedience in the same direction" focus in our lives.[6]

In the earlier passage we examined from Philippians 3, Paul spells out his focused goal for his life: to know and become like Christ. He goes on to talk about the priority this ambition has for him. He recognizes he hasn't attained what he's pursuing and that he isn't perfect, but he says, "*One thing* I do. . . . I press on toward the goal for the prize" (vv. 13–14, emphasis added). Deep focus and clear priorities govern what Paul does and doesn't do, and even what he does when obstacles and hardships appear.

6. Eugene Peterson has a book of this name based on a quotation from Friedrich Nietzsche.

Amy Carmichael was one of these individuals with a clear ambition to live for God's kingdom.[7] She grew up and was raised in Northern Ireland in a Christian home. During college and young adulthood, she discovered a passion and desire to help working-class girls suffering great poverty. Her care for the poor and the vulnerable eventually expanded into a burden for the needy and outcast in places like India, China, and Japan. Compelled by a calling and passion to serve them by sharing God's love and grace in Jesus, Amy was sent to India by the Church of England Zenana Missionary Society.

After Amy had spent five years in India, with seemingly little fruit to show for her work, a small 7-year-old girl came to Amy's missionary compound seeking refuge. This was how Amy learned of the Indian practice of families selling their young daughters to the local Hindu gods as temple prostitutes. Amy's ambition from that moment on was to rescue as many children as she could from the darkness of immorality, exploitation, and murder. She started the Dohnavur Fellowship, a ministry to at-risk children providing housing, care, education, and spiritual development in Western India.

The ministry wasn't easy or painless for Amy. Living in India and facing the spiritual and physical opposition of the kingdom of darkness was no simple thing. Yet she endured and persevered for more than 50 years, never returning home, even for a ministry leave. She saw

7. For details of Amy Carmichael's life and ministry, see Tim Keesee, *A Company of Heroes: Portraits from the Gospel's Global Advance* (Crossway, 2019); J. D. Douglas with Philip W. Comfort and Donald Mitchell, eds., *Who's Who in Christian History* (Tyndale House, 1992).

ministry like a soldier, as a battle God called her to fight. In one of her books, she wrote,

> More has been written about the successes than about the failures, and it seems to us that it is more important that you should know about the reverses than about the successes of the war. *We shall have all eternity to celebrate the victories, but we have only the few hours before sunset in which to win them.*[8]

Amy knew she must focus her time, energy, and attention and make it her priority to continue laboring for the gospel despite hardships and difficulties.

3. Perspiration

A third element necessary for endurance through hardship is what I'll call "perspiration." I'm referring to the reality that enduring hardship requires effort and hard work. Remember Paul's grand ambition to know and be like Christ? A lofty aim, it doesn't happen overnight or by passively laying back and hoping Christ will be known and formed in us. While the gospel message tells us life in Christ is entirely a gift, "grace-driven effort"[9] must be expended toward becoming who we are in Christ.

Paul sums it up when he talks about this aim of his life and then says, "One thing I do: forgetting what lies behind and *straining* forward to what lies ahead, *I press on* toward the goal of the prize of the upward call of God in

8. Keesee, *A Company of Heroes*, 209. Emphasis mine.
9. See Carson, *For the Love of God*, 49.

Christ Jesus" (Phil. 3:13–14, emphasis added). In the metaphors of endurance that Paul speaks to Timothy about, he encourages him to consider the "hard-working farmer" (2 Tim. 2:6). The Christian life and the pursuit of ambitions for Christ, his kingdom, and the good of our fellow humans will not come through passive concern. To do anything for the kingdom is a matter of hard work, diligence, and perseverance. The writer of Hebrews calls us to "lay aside every weight, and sin which clings so closely, and let us run with endurance the race that is set before us" (Heb. 12:1).

When you evaluate the success of ending human slave trafficking in the mid-19th century and the advancements of the American civil rights movement of the 1950s and '60s, men and women of staggering character emerge. Among them, figures like William Wilberforce, Harriet Tubman, Mary McLeod Bethune, Martin Luther King Jr., and John M. Perkins labored tirelessly to see the end of slavery, segregation, and the oppressive treatment of human beings created in God's image. Perkins relates in his book *One Blood*, "We simply cannot do the hard work of reconciliation without great commitment. This work is hard, and the forces of evil are engaged to prevent it from happening."[10]

Such hard work and willingness to suffer hardship and persevere have allowed for great strides in realizing the aims of human dignity, social equity, and just reconciliation.

10. John M. Perkins and Karen Waddles, *One Blood: Parting Words to the Church on Race and Love* (Moody, 2018), 23.

4. Power

While the prior three elements are necessary, they may appear to call us to bear down, work harder, try better, and never give up. You could find this advice in any secular leadership training. These guides make focus, discipline, and hard work the keys to accomplishing your goals and achieving your ambitions. When we talk about spiritual ambitions, however, we can't merely rely on the wider world's strategies and efforts. God has to empower our work, or we labor and strive in vain (Ps. 127:1). The power of the Holy Spirit himself must be at work within us to enable our endurance in hardship.

Paul often mentioned the nature of his ministry when he wrote to various churches. In writing to the Colossian believers, he told them, "I have become [the church's] servant, according to God's commission that was given to me for you, to make the word of God fully known" (Col. 1:25, CSB). To fulfill that commission, Paul began preaching and teaching the gospel "so that [he could] present everyone mature in Christ" (v. 28, CSB). But how did he go about this? How did he accomplish his aim of making Jesus known? He tells us, "I labor for this, striving *with his strength that works powerfully* in me" (v. 29, CSB, emphasis added). The dynamic here is powerful. Paul has his perspectives and priorities dialed in. He knows he has to work hard and press on. But all these efforts are contingent on the Spirit supplying the strength necessary for persevering in ministry.

In another place, the apostle Peter challenges us, "If anyone serves, let it be from the strength God provides, so that God may be glorified through Christ Jesus in everything" (1 Pet. 4:11, CSB). Our efforts and attempts to serve the Lord, advance the gospel, and love our neighbors well rely on doing so by the power that God supplies. This means we must be humble and ask God to sustain and strengthen us. When the Spirit empowers our work, we can endure hardship well.

Gifted Endurance

The Bible is filled with examples of men and women with glorious ambitions. They wanted to do as missionary William Carey said: "Expect great things from God. Attempt great things for God."[11] They knew what they were called to and had the drive and focus to clarify their mission. They worked, taught, served, gave, suffered, and sacrificed greatly for their individual callings. They accomplished great things because God's Spirit empowered them. We could walk through Hebrews 11 name by name and see the pattern clearly.

Yet only one name is provided to us as the supreme model *and* victor: Jesus Christ. The culmination of the "Great Hall of Faith" in Hebrews 11 leads us to Hebrews 12:1–2, where we're encouraged,

> Therefore, since we are surrounded by so great a cloud of witnesses, let us also lay aside every weight, and sin which clings so closely, and *let us run with endurance* the race that is set before us, *looking to Jesus*, the founder and perfecter of our faith, who for the

11. S. Pearce Carey and Peter Masters, *William Carey: The Father of Modern Missions* (Wakeman Trust, 1993), 77.

> joy that was set before him *endured* the cross, despising the shame, and is seated at the right hand of the throne of God. (emphasis added)

Jesus is the One who ran his race with endurance perfectly. He's the One who "set his face to go to Jerusalem" (Luke 9:51), knowing the cross was his destiny and suffering was his vocation. He went willingly, he suffered a brutal death, and he endured on our behalf. Victory—including our forgiveness and acceptance by God—was secured by Jesus's work of suffering hardship in our place. It's not because of our own work but because of the active obedience of Jesus Christ in his life, death, and resurrection. Jesus secures everything for us through his steadfast labor, and there isn't one work we can bring or add to improve his work.

The writer of Hebrews calls us to look to Jesus, not just as an example for our perseverance but as the One who has pioneered and perfected our faith (12:2). Making it your ambition to endure hardship results from receiving the gift of Jesus's perfect work through his endurance and suffering. He has secured every benefit, blessing, and victory. Because of this, we can endeavor great and good things by faith, knowing that Christ has forever secured our achievement. We can endure hardship because the result of Christ's hardship is already victory.

Discussion Questions

1. What place does perseverance and endurance have in our culture today? Would you say endurance, or "doing hard things," is valued?

2. Why is enduring hardship necessary for the Christian life?
3. Where do your perspectives, priorities, "perspirations," and sources of power need to grow or change so you can achieve great pursuits for God?
4. How does Jesus's own suffering and endurance enable and inspire us in our own?
5. What would your life look like if you made it your ambition to endure hardship?

7

Make It Your Ambition to Serve Vocationally in Christian Leadership

I don't think Chris had it in mind to be a pastor. He went to school to study business and stock trading. Steve was a premedical student plugging away at his studies, not thinking about leading a student ministry. Ashley was working on her law degree. Today, she serves with a major international Christian ministry in Japan. David was a physician with distinction. Lauded as one of the most brilliant young physicians of his day, he left the medical field and began pastoring in a small, poor mining community.[1] William was a shoemaker in a small town who uprooted his family to India and translated the Bible into

1. D. E. Davies, "David Martyn Lloyd-Jones" in *Biographical Dictionary of Evangelicals*, ed. Timothy Larsen et al. (IVP, 2003), 371.

more than 30 languages.[2] Lily was an aspiring painter and artist. She put her successful art career aside to move to Northern Africa and reach communities of Muslim women that the men couldn't access.[3] Bill was an economics student and entrepreneur who started his own candy company. After becoming a Christian, he sold his business and started a campus ministry at the local university that later became one of the largest parachurch organizations in the world.[4]

All these people had a given trajectory and direction for their lives. Good and noble vocations were in front of them. Yet each one of them ended up serving vocationally in Christian leadership. If you'd asked them when they were young if they could envision being pastors, global missionaries, or leaders in Christian organizations and ministries, they probably would've laughed. Yet God called them into full-time Christian service. They weren't leaving ungodly secular occupations in exchange for sacred and holy roles. They were simply following God's call on their lives to serve him in specific roles within Christian ministry. They surrendered their ambitions and life trajectories to pursue new and God-given ambitions—with worldwide, eternal effects.

In this chapter, I want to return to the two questions I introduced you to at the beginning of this book: *What do you want to do when you grow up, and what will you do for the kingdom of God?* I raise these questions again because

2. James P. Eckman, *Exploring Church History* (Crossway, 2002), 79.
3. Russ Ramsey, *Rembrandt Is in the Wind: Learning to Love Art through the Eyes of Faith* (Zondervan, 2022), 204–206.
4. K. L. Staggers, "Bright, William ('Bill') Rohl," Daniel G. Reid et al., *Dictionary of Christianity in America* (IVP, 1990).

I want to challenge you to a final ambition as you think about your answers. You may be pursuing a particular career path or occupation. You may be enrolled in a degree program right now, with plans to graduate, find a job, and head into your future with a career that puts food on the table and gives you something to do with your time. There's nothing wrong with that. But is influence for God's kingdom a driving factor in your plans?

After encouraging you to set your life's trajectory toward Christ and serving him and his people, I want to sum all this up with one final ambition. If the prior six ambitions have rung true for your life—and I hope they have—there's one more great ambition to pursue. *Make it your ambition to serve vocationally in Christian leadership.* If you're pursuing knowing and loving God (ambition #1), modeling Christ's character (ambition #2), developing your gifts and using them to serve (ambition #3), charting out a career path aimed at serving others (ambition #4), sharing the gospel of Christ (ambition #5), and enduring hardship and difficulty (ambition #6), then you should definitely consider a vocation in Christian leadership and ministry. You should pursue serving vocationally in a local church as a ministry leader, director, or pastor. You should consider taking your skills and gifts and living in a different culture and location as a missionary. Have you given thought to a career with a parachurch ministry or organization?

This possibility may have never seriously crossed your mind. You may have thought going into Christian ministry is something *other* people do. But I invite you to consider full-time Christian ministry. Try to envision spending the best years of your life ahead pastoring a local church, serving on staff with a Christian organization, or seeking to make disciples of Jesus in a foreign context. To help you envision this life and pursue this ambition, I'm going to expose you to the need for laborers in ministry, help you understand the calling to serve in ministry, and explore the joy and eternal blessings that exist for those in ministry. If these resonate with you, you should make it your ambition to serve vocationally in Christian ministry.

Who Will Lead in the Next Generation?

It's no secret there has been a significant religious shift in our society in the last 25 years. Recent studies have shown that some 40 million Americans have stopped attending church on a weekly basis. One significant research project reported, "More people have left the church in the last twenty-five years than all the new people who became Christians from the First Great Awakening, Second Great Awakening, and Billy Graham crusades combined."[5] With this kind of shift and the continued trajectory of more dechurching, the effects on Christian churches, educational institutions, mission organizations, and denominational entities will be deeply felt. Beyond churches closing, losing supporting members means fewer financial resources for church planting, global missions, mercy ministries, and higher education and training.[6] If you zoom out beyond churches and

5. Jim Davis and Michael S. Graham with Ryan P. Burge, *The Great Dechurching: Who's Leaving, Why Are They Going, and What Will It Take to Bring Them Back?* (Zondervan, 2023), 5.
6. Davis, Graham, and Burge, *The Great Dechurching*, 12.

Christian institutions, the loss "will invariably diminish resources that provide relief, care, and aid to the poor, disenfranchised, sick, hurting, and otherwise needy."[7] The outlook is bleak, with this kind of movement resulting in "diminished human flourishing, connectivity, cohesiveness, and overall shalom"[8] in our society.

Practically, this means there'll be fewer churches, fewer global mission agencies, fewer Christian nonprofit organizations, and fewer Christian colleges, universities, and seminaries if the trend continues. We'll have fewer Christian book publishers, service and relief organizations, and recovery ministries and shelters. Overall, Christianity in America is in remarkable decline, and the effects will be felt in many communities.

When you look at the movement of people away from the church, there's another troubling trend: the average age of pastors and Christian leaders. One study in 2020 found the median age of congregational leaders is 57 years old,[9] which was seven years older than the same study done in 2000. The leaders of the local church are getting older while teens and young adults are leaving the church. In the coming decades, there'll be a religious generation gap between leaders and the majority population.

On paper, these trends don't generate hope and excitement for Christianity's future. However, these

7. Davis, Graham, and Burge, *The Great Dechurching*, 19.
8. Davis, Graham, and Burge, *The Great Dechurching*, 20.
9. "Twenty Years of Congregational Change: The 2020 Faith Communities Today Overview," (Hartford Institute for Religion Research, 2021), https://faithcommunitiestoday.org/wp-content/uploads/2021/10/Faith-Communities-Today-2020-Summary-Report.pdf.

studies tell me one thing: the next 25 years are critical years to equip, disciple, and deploy the next generation of gospel laborers. If the number of qualified men and women going into vocational Christian leadership declines, so will those institutions' relative strength and effectiveness. We need a new generation of called, equipped, and deployed men and women who will be a leadership catalyst for the Christian faith in our society.

We must also look beyond the data and analysis. Jesus encouraged his followers to consider the spiritual needs and conditions of the communities around us. Jesus did this in his own context—the Gospel writer Matthew observed, "When he saw the crowds, he had compassion for them, because they were harassed and helpless, like sheep without a shepherd" (Matt. 9:36). Do the spiritual condition and the needs of those around us prompt any compassion and empathy in our hearts? If you think about the next 25 years of your life and consider Christianity's trajectory, do you feel concerned for the eternal well-being of the people around you?

This concern prompted Jesus to challenge his disciples to take action—not at first to go into ministry but to pray: "Then he said to his disciples, 'The harvest is plentiful, but the laborers are few; therefore pray earnestly to the Lord of the harvest to send out laborers into his harvest'" (vv. 37–38). Just like in our day, where there's a great need for gospel ministry, there's a corresponding need for qualified "laborers" who will enter the fields of ministry to serve the Lord. Yet Jesus doesn't say, "Hey, big need, better get out there." He calls his disciples to pray regarding the need and whom the Lord will send.

If this chapter prompts you to do anything in your life, would it at least be a commitment to pray for the supply, support, and strength of those serving in vocational Christian ministry? I hope you'll become a person who asks God to prompt and provide the gospel laborers needed in this moment and in the years to come. Pray!

When You're Compelled to Do More than Pray

As you pray, you might find a disruptive "holy discontentment"[10] in your heart about the need for gospel ministers and your part in answering that need. The divine design of the Lord often leads those who pray about certain needs to become the means by which he answers that need. Indeed, the disciples who were encouraged to pray for laborers for the harvest became the laborers sent to the harvest. After Jesus gave the Great Commission, the Twelve and others dispersed from Jerusalem carrying the message of the resurrected Lord to the ends of the earth. When you're praying and wrestling with the need for Christian workers, you may become convicted to answer that need personally. How then would you know if that impulse is God's call on your life to serve or just a momentary interest that comes to you?

To help you make it your ambition to serve the Lord in Christian ministry, you need to understand what constitutes an authentic calling by God to Christian service and vocational ministry. Throughout the Bible, God sets

10. One of my pastoral mentors, Steve Fernandez, used that phrase when discussing men and women trying to discern their desires and ambitions regarding ministry.

apart many prophets, disciples, evangelists, apostles, and leaders for the work of Christian ministry. The testimony of countless men and women serving in ministry through the generations echoes and affirms God's calling and commissioning of individuals to serve him. How would you know if that's you?

Many have attempted to answer this question well, and many good resources delve into the issue of discerning a calling to Christian ministry.[11] Still, I'd like to identify five signposts for a call to ministry. As I tried to answer that question for myself years ago, I stumbled on a letter that one pastor, John Newton (of "Amazing Grace" fame), wrote to a younger man wrestling with the same question. Newton knew how many struggle to discern if they're called to ministry and wrote, "My first desires toward the ministry were attended with great uncertainties and difficulties, and the perplexity of my own mind was heightened by the various and opposite judgments of my friends."[12] Yet he understood what makes for a true calling and followed the Lord in it. These five signposts stand the test of time to help us as well.

1. Desire to Lead in Ministry

Paul told Timothy that one of the first qualifications for a man who'd be an elder or pastor in the church is a desire

11. I recommend *Am I Called?* by Dave Harvey (Crossway, 2012), *Discerning Your Call to Ministry* by Jason K. Allen (Moody, 2016), and Charles H. Spurgeon's lecture "The Call to Ministry" in his volume *Lectures to My Students* (Banner of Truth, 2008).
12. John Newton and Richard Cecil, *The Works of John Newton*, vol. 2 (London, 1824), 44.

to serve in that capacity: "The saying is trustworthy: If anyone aspires to the office of overseer, he desires a noble task" (1 Tim. 3:1). Peter instructs the elders of the early church, "Shepherd God's flock among you, not overseeing out of compulsion but willingly, as God would have you" (1 Pet. 5:2, CSB). Leading in ministry shouldn't be a matter of obligation or of someone forcing you to do it, as if you have no agency or decision-making power. The best leaders in Christian ministry are the ones who want to be in leadership.

Newton, in his letter to his young friend, said, "I apprehend, the man who is once moved by the Spirit of God to this work [Christian ministry], will prefer it, if attainable, to thousands of gold and silver; so that, though he is at times intimidated by a sense of its importance and difficulty, compared with his own great insufficiency . . . yet he cannot give it up."[13]

I want to stress that this desire is a *starting* signpost. It's not the sum of all the marks of a calling. But if you have even a small piquing interest in serving in Christian ministry, you're in a position where a calling to serve vocationally might be a valid call from God.

Here's a specific word for young men: Consider pastoral ministry or even a lay elder role in your local church as a "noble task." Expressing interest in or a desire to be a pastor is good and worthy, and it's not wrong to lean into fulfilling that desire. The church needs godly, humble, wise, and zealous men to lead its mission with clear direction and spiritual maturity. We need young men to aim their lives toward the noble task of shepherding the

13. Newton and Cecil, *The Works of John Newton*, 44–45.

church. This may mean entering into pastoral ministry vocationally, or it may mean pursuing leadership in your local church as a lay elder—able to work in vocation but also serving the church as an unpaid elder. Men, the church in the next decades will need more godly leaders to step up and "shepherd God's flock among you." If that interest is at all in your heart, don't squelch it, but pray and pursue it for the glory of God and the well-being of his people.

2. Competency to Lead in Ministry

Beyond your desires, you need a corresponding capability and competency to labor vocationally in Christian ministry. You need to develop and grow in the qualifications and abilities required to carry out the ministry you're called to. It'd be absurd for me to claim to be called to be a Christian musician when I can't play an instrument and my family questions if I can hold a tune when we sing together at church. I need to gain the competency to lead in that area. However, there are other competencies for ministry that I possess and have developed so I'm qualified to serve as a pastor at my local church.

Before you ever attain the ability to "do the job," the bigger question of competency is whether you have the character that qualifies you to serve in the role. As you recall, in chapter 2, we identified that character matters. Having the high character of a man or woman who's above reproach is a prerequisite to being vocationally engaged in ministry. We represent the Lord as his ambassadors in ministry and, therefore, should reflect Christ's glorious character and integrity (2 Cor. 5:20).

It may feel out of step to say you must be competent in the relevant character and abilities of Christ to know you're called to Christian ministry, especially if you're young and seeking to discern this calling for your life. Again, Newton offers helpful encouragement. He says these competencies "are to appear in due season: they are not to be expected instantaneously, but gradually, in the use of proper means. They are necessary for the discharge of the ministry; but not necessary as pre-requisites to warrant our desires after it. In your case, you are young and have time before you."[14] These competencies of character and ability are something you can pray for, pursue, and grow in as you make it your ambition to serve vocationally in Christian leadership.

3. Community Affirmation

The long-running reality show *American Idol* involves the search for aspiring singers to develop and promote to stardom throughout the course of a season. The best (and most cringey) episodes are the early audition rounds where anyone can apply and sing before a panel of judges, some of whom are downright brutal. It never fails that every season at the audition stage, several applicants can't carry a tune in a bucket. When the judges tell them, "No way!" their dreams are crushed. What often discourages them so much is that someone (usually a well-meaning relative) told them they're a great singer. When they came to the panel of industry experts who know music, they're shocked to learn that

14. Newton and Cecil, *The Works of John Newton*, 45.

the affirmation they'd received back home isn't equaled by affirmation from experts and authorities. Sometimes we think we're called and competent to do something merely because a well-meaning friend told us we're great at it, but we're not.

This third signpost of community affirmation is essential to help you discern a calling to ministry. But it doesn't mean only asking your favorite aunt or your best friend if they think you'd be great in Christian leadership (go ahead and ask them—they'll say yes). You need to ask the right people to speak about your ambitions and career trajectory. Those right people are the spiritual leaders and community of your local church. Do your pastors and elders see a desire to serve and an ability to do that? Can those discipling you affirm a trajectory toward Christian ministry? If so, then moving forward in pursuit of the next signpost is valid. If you're considering pastoral ministry, this affirmation may involve an ordination process led by local church or denominational leadership. Either way, it'd be best if you allowed rightful leadership and the Christian community to speak into your life and trajectory of calling.

4. Open Doors to Serve Vocationally

Have you been offered a ministry job to serve in? Has someone or an organization extended openness or an invitation for you to take a role to meet a need on your heart? This signpost of a calling in ministry is essential because it requires our dependence on the Lord's direction and invitation into a place. We may have desires and ambitions, but the Lord directs our steps and opens and closes doors. Waiting at this signpost can be frustrating and make us impatient, but asking the Lord to open the doors to fulfill what we've desired and been equipped and affirmed for is an act of profound humility to trust his wise and good providence for our lives.

Newton spoke to his young friend about this by saying, "If it be the Lord's will to bring you into his ministry, he has already appointed your place and service; and though you know it not at present, you shall at a proper time. If you had the talents of an angel, you could do no good with them till his hour is come, and till he leads you to the people whom he has determined to bless by your means."[15] If the Lord calls you to serve him vocationally in Christian leadership, he'll open the door to that end.

5. Compulsion to Serve

A final signpost to discerning a calling into Christian leadership is similar to the first, yet it's deeper than just desire. Some have used the term "unction" to describe this signpost. It's the internal work of God's Spirit in your life to make you utterly unsatisfied doing anything else. Charles Spurgeon famously told the students of his Pastors' College, "Do not enter the ministry *if you can help it*."[16] He wasn't saying that to douse water on the hot fires of these students' ambitions and desires or to paint the picture that ministry wasn't worth going into. He identified that there must be a Holy Spirit–given compulsion

15. Newton and Cecil, *The Works of John Newton*, 46.
16. C. H. Spurgeon, *Lectures to My Students: A Selection from Addresses Delivered to the Students of the Pastors' College, Metropolitan Tabernacle*, vol. 1 (London, 1875), 23. Emphasis original.

within you that says, *I must serve the Lord this way*. Spurgeon went on to say, "If on the other hand, you can say that for all the wealth of [the world] you could not and dare not espouse any other calling so as to be put aside from preaching the gospel of Jesus Christ, then, depend upon it, if other things be equally satisfactory, you have the signs of this apostleship."[17]

Paul spoke of this compulsion from the Lord by saying, "For Christ's love compels us, because we are convinced that one died for all" (2 Cor. 5:14, NIV). That compelling, compulsive desire to spend your life in vocational Christian ministry may feel like a tipping point between obedience and disobedience to the Lord. Nevertheless, it's an all-out *must* for your life.

One crucial reality about this signpost must be considered along with all the others. This final signpost can help you discern if you're called to Christian ministry only because the prior four signposts are already true. This is also why it's similar to the first signpost, desire. You may desire something, but this is the God-given internal compulsion based on your desire, character, competency, community affirmation, and God-given opportunity to serve that culminates with a holy necessity to carry out this work.

Ministry of Glory

One of the reservations I've heard many express about going into ministry is that the difficulty and disappointments of Christian leadership are heavy to carry. The

17. Spurgeon, *Lectures to My Students*, 23.

drop-out and moral failure rate of those who started in ministry roles is high. The deep pains of church hurt and the discouragement of working with sinners and trying to help them become like Christ can't be avoided or brushed aside. These agonies are real, and they're part of the calling. Take a few minutes to consider Paul's own experience of shipwreck, danger, "toil and hardship, through many a sleepless night, in hunger and thirst, often without food, in cold and exposure" (2 Cor. 11:27) and you'll quickly become aware of the challenges that serving vocationally in ministry will bring. Yet Paul didn't wilt or bemoan his ministry as if it were a punishment for being a willing Christian. Paul saw the ministry of the gospel as a greater privilege and calling. He asked, "Will not the ministry of the Spirit have even more glory?" (3:8).

When you think of the myriad of things you could do with your life, does the list of options before you have any "glory" in it? Do your ambitions have anything in them that lives beyond the average 70 or 80 years of life we're allotted (Ps. 90:10)? Laboring in vocational Christian ministry isn't the only way to have an eternal influence, but it contains some of the greatest potential for this.

I don't know how our ministry's fruitfulness will be judged as we sojourn to the kingdom of heaven, but I'm eager for the work I've done in this life to yield a great harvest in eternity. I'm hopeful that the sermons I've preached, the hours I've counseled, the initiatives I've organized, the articles and books I've written, the non-Christians I've witnessed to, and the effort I've expended to see Jesus Christ lifted up as the Savior and

King over all will yield fruit in eternity. I hold hope in the promise that Peter gave to fellow elders when he called us to shepherd the flock of God: "When the chief Shepherd appears, you will receive the unfading crown of glory" (1 Pet. 5:4).

Friend, the need is great, and the calling is glorious. I want you to do something great and glorious for the Lord. I want you to give yourself to benefit God's kingdom. Jesus is worth all we have and all we do. Imagine the difference for Christ's cause that could be made in the next 25 years if you and those of your generation made it your ambition to serve Christ vocationally in Christian leadership. May the Lord send laborers into his harvest! May it be you.

Discussion Questions

1. Have you ever given thought to being a pastor, ministry director, missionary, or leader in a Christian ministry organization? Why or why not?
2. How would you answer the question "Who will lead the next generation?" How can you answer that need?
3. What would you say to someone who desires to go into ministry but doesn't possess the character or competency for ministry? How could you encourage him or her?
4. What might be a barrier or obstacle keeping you from pursuing vocational ministry as a career?
5. What would your life look like if you made it your ambition to vocationally serve in Christian leadership?

Making Your Ambitions Reality

As I left the Moody Church auditorium on a bitterly cold February evening, I knew my life's trajectory was about to change. I'd heard sermons before, many by some of the best and most sought-after preachers of the day. But this one was different. This sermon on God's glory and all things being "from him and through him and to him" (Rom. 11:36) resonated within me. The preacher was a renowned and respected pastor who'd led a faithful ministry. Yet it wasn't the preacher's charisma or eloquence that affected my heart. During the sermon, I had an impression I can only attribute to the Holy Spirit. I didn't hear an audible voice from heaven while James Montgomery Boice preached on the glory of God. Yet I sensed the Lord whispering, "Do you see what he's doing proclaiming my glory through my Word? This is what I want *you* to do too. I want you to become a pastor and preach the Bible wherever I send you."

More than 25 years later, I'm doing it. I'm pastoring and preaching. On Sunday mornings, I open my Bible and do my best to share God's glory and grace with everyone who gathers with us for worship. During the week, I lead the ministry staff, disciple men, counsel church members, pray with the hurting, compile sermon research documents, and follow through on a host of other responsibilities involved with leading a local church. While I haven't attained perfection or completed the race set before me, I've come to a point where the questions I was once asking about my future and my vocational pursuits have been answered. I'm seeking to fulfill the ambitions the Lord has given me well to serve and honor him.

Through this book, I've been laying before you a series of pursuits to help give trajectory and definition to your life as an adult and follower of Jesus. My goal has been to encourage you to live your life for God's glory and the building of his kingdom. If you take another look at the first six pursuits, you'll find a trajectory for life that every Christian should embrace. If you're chasing after those targets, the final pursuit of a career or vocation in Christian ministry could be the natural next step. If you're curious about entering vocational Christian ministry or how to approach taking that step toward it, I want to help you practically put this all together in this chapter. If there isn't a desire in your heart or a sense of calling to step into Christian ministry, that's OK. I've written an epilogue to provide specific encouragement for you about your next steps. For now, let's explore the three necessary elements required to make your potential ministry ambitions a reality.

You Need Christian Community

If you're going into vocational Christian ministry, you'll need to be a member of a local church. I want to stress this for two reasons. First, the spiritual body and community of the Christian faith is the church. Jesus didn't start food pantries, mission agencies, publishers, or hospitals. He established local assemblies of his people under morally qualified and competent leaders, and these assemblies are called the church. As the people of the church are sent into the world, they go and work, some even establishing great Christian institutions and parachurch ministries. However, these organizations aren't replacements for the local church. It's a paradox for a Christian to be "in ministry" yet not a member of a local church.

A second reason it's necessary to be a member of a local church is so you can be influenced and directed by the local body of Christ as you explore a future in ministry. Pastors, teachers, and mentors will all be instrumental in your formation and in the support and affirmation of your gifts, talents, and calling to serve in vocational ministry. If you have a large network of friends, roommates, and colleagues outside of a church context, you may assume you have an adequate base of community. Still, like the *American Idol* contestants I mentioned in the last chapter, you may only have an echo chamber around you saying what you want to hear. Instead, you need godly, wise, and experienced leaders to speak into your life.

In the New Testament, a practice called "the laying on of hands" is mentioned several times when church leaders commission and validate properly called people to act as ministers for the gospel. The leaders physically place their hands on these new ministers in an act of affirmation and send them to the work the Lord has called them to. The first leaders set apart to serve the daily distribution of bread were commissioned by the apostles through prayer and the laying on of hands (Acts 6:6). Paul and Barnabas were sent from the church in Antioch to plant churches after the elders there laid their hands on them and prayed over them (13:3). Timothy was reminded in a letter from Paul that the elders had laid their hands on him and commissioned him for ministry (1 Tim. 4:14). Likewise, Paul stressed that Timothy shouldn't be too quick to appoint or ordain other leaders without making sure they're properly called and qualified for that ministry (5:22).

I draw this out because if you're making it your ambition to serve vocationally in Christian ministry, you shouldn't proceed without the affirmation, blessing, and even ordination of your local church's elders and leaders. There might be staff members, board members, or other key leaders in a Christian organization that isn't a church who affirm your calling and gifting. Still, leadership authority for Christian ministry should come from the affirmation and encouragement of the church first and foremost.

Being a member of a local church will help keep you in bounds while serving Christ and advancing the gospel. Many times, I've observed men and women deciding to be independent "free agent" ministers, eschewing authority and oversight, believing they can do it better or more effectively without the oversight of church leaders.

Usually, they end up making a wreck of themselves and doing significant damage to others and to the testimony of Christ in the process. It was a trademark move of the first century's false teachers to "[go] on ahead" of the leadership and teaching of the gospel (2 John 9).

If you still live at home, I'll assume you're already connected to a local church and encourage you to continue gathering and growing there. If you're in a new community due to attending college or university, look for a good church that preaches the Bible, faithfully communicates the gospel, and has qualified leaders you can learn from and be mentored by. The Gospel Coalition has a directory of churches on its website that can help you locate and connect with a local church in a new city.[1] Don't substitute the campus ministries you might attend, like Cru or Navigators, as your "church." Be sure to connect with a local gathering of the saints, not just students from your college campus.

You Need Training and Development

If you're going to turn your aspiration into a reality, you'll also need to be equipped with the skills and experiences that are part of Christian ministry. In some circles, the idea of a vocational clergy or career ministry is looked down on. After all, doesn't Ephesians 4 teach that every church member is to serve as a minister? Echoing the GEICO commercial of yesteryear, Christian ministry is viewed as something "so easy, a caveman could do it."

1. Search the TGC Church Directory at https://www.thegospelcoalition.org/churches/.

Some point to pastors like D. L. Moody or Spurgeon as examples of leaders who never had a formal degree or attended seminary. While that may have been the experience of a few, most (if not all) would benefit from and find necessary a season of focused training in Christian ministry. Even Paul had 3 to 14 years of training and development before he was sent with Barnabas to plant churches (Gal. 1:11–2:1).

Depending on the kind of ministry you intend to enter, the training you'll need will vary. For those interested in serving as a pastor or ministry leader, specifically in teaching the Bible, a master's degree in biblical and theological studies would be needed at the very least, if not a master's degree in divinity (MDiv). Theological programs of study seek to equip students with the robust tools of understanding, interpreting, and teaching the Bible to help others learn what it means and how it applies to life today. Seminaries and Christian universities teach a theological framework (sometimes called a system) for making sense of the whole Bible and being able to address the nuances of specific topics. Good MDiv programs also educate and train in preaching, pastoral counsel and care, and church leadership. Because these degree programs are at the master's level, you'll find most undergraduate degrees will fulfill the prerequisites to advance to an MDiv program. If you're in the undergraduate phase of your education, consider looking into free courses and online training to help you grow your biblical fluency and aptitude before going to seminary. The Gospel Coalition offers many free online courses covering biblical, historical, theological, and practical studies.[2]

Depending on the kind of work you're doing in global missions or parachurch ministry locally, you should explore training in a vocation similar to a nonministry role here in the United States. For instance, premed and medical school training is essential if you're considering medical missions. If you're working in education, completing a degree in education and instruction is appropriate. Attending a Christian college or university is optional to prepare for these roles. However, they can be helpful institutions for gaining ministry focus and biblical development to accompany your regular studies. You may not know what you're headed into, but in general, having a degree in a specific field will equip you to be more competent in the ministry you're called to.

At this season in your life, you don't have to know your precise and complete destination, but by pointing yourself in a direction, you'll gain the necessary skills and perspectives to help you lead and serve in the future in Christian ministry.

You Need Ministry Experience

Weight lifters love the concept of "reps." Through their repetitive and frequent lifts, they're developing strength in body parts where they want more muscle. Similarly, getting practice in ministry will help you develop "spiritual muscle." In taking your next steps toward serving

2. Browse all TGC's free online courses at https://www.thegospelcoalition.org/courses/.

and leading in Christian ministry, you're going to need boots-on-the-ground experience. This may sound counterintuitive, like a fast-food chain requiring their cooks to have three to five years of experience as an executive chef in a fine restaurant. However, ministry opportunities and experiences abound and can help clarify a calling without you needing to commit fully to or long-term immerse yourself in that field.

When I first enrolled at Moody Bible Institute, I declared global missions as my major. I'd already been on several overseas short-term mission trips in high school and was influenced by the stories of Jim Elliot and the four other missionaries who'd died trying to take the gospel to the Auca people in the remote jungles of Ecuador. I already had a deep desire to serve in ministry, so I assumed this was the logical path forward. As I entered my first year of studies in the missions department, I started recognizing I wasn't as interested in the coursework as much as I'd previously envisioned. Sitting through an anthropology class wasn't interesting or exciting to me. On that cold February night of Boice's sermon, I sensed I should change my major and pursue a degree in pastoral studies. Preaching and teaching the Bible felt more alive to me than anything. Yet before I changed my major, I knew I needed to "feel it out" and see if this was a wise and accurate shift for me. I needed the affirmation of my pastors and leaders, as well as good training. This led me to inquire within my home church about a summer internship with the middle-school ministry.

During that internship, I found ministry in the local church exciting and engaging. I experienced the day-to-day responsibilities of being a youth pastor. I was affirmed in my desire to change my major to pastoral studies, encouraged in my giftings (underdeveloped as they were), and challenged to think through future steps to pursue the pastoral calling.

If you're considering vocational ministry, I'd highly recommend gaining practical experience through internships, ministry residencies, short-term mission trips, and even leading and teaching in ordinary church ministries, among other development avenues. The church where I now serve as a pastor (Woodside Bible Church in southeast Michigan) has a Leadership Institute that takes on several paid residents for 12 to 24 months to give practical experience and leadership development so they can clarify their calling, develop their gifts, and prepare for serving the Lord vocationally in the church or beyond. A host of other churches, organizations, and opportunities exist for you to gain practical experience in ministry.

Take the Next Step

I didn't come into pastoral ministry overnight. My calling to pastor and preach didn't mean I landed in the pastorate as soon as I walked out of Moody Church that February evening. It was a process of years of development, training, opportunities, disappointments, and open doors to serve. My encouragement is to not set your expectations that you'll have it all worked out as soon as you close this book. However, I want you to adopt the long-road perspective and begin taking steps, even today, to pursue God and move toward his calling on your life. You might not know exactly what to do next or where to go. This is why the three preparation elements I mentioned above are essential. Reach out to one of your pastors, a small group leader, or someone you know in Christian ministry. Begin discussing these ambitions and aspirations with them. The church community can help you determine the next steps you might take.

Additionally, begin praying and asking the Lord to give you clarity, passion, and direction for this potential ministry future. This is the most important thing we can do when considering the future. Praying is an act of dependence and an expression of your trust in God's love for you. He'll be generous in giving you the wisdom and direction you desire, especially as you sense his call in your life. Pray and ask that "God may open to [you] a door for the word" (Col. 4:3). As you pray, push on doors. Ask for opportunities to serve in areas you may feel called to or desire. If the door is closed or the answer is no, be encouraged that the Lord is simply directing your steps elsewhere.

Whether you're called to serve in a ministry vocation or not, take the next steps of knowing and loving God. Not one day of your life will be wasted, misspent, or lost in the pursuit of knowing and being found in Christ. Being known, loved, and made new in him is worth more than anything and everything this world has to offer. The influence and flourishing of the gospel will be unmatched if your generation will give yourselves to making the glory of God and the gospel of Jesus your greatest ambition. Make it your ambition to be an influence for the kingdom.

Discussion Questions

1. What resonated with you in this chapter?
2. Why is being a member of a local church necessary for your development and success in pursuing vocational ministry? How are you involved in your local church?
3. Where do you need to take steps for training and ministry development?
4. How and where can you get experience in vocational ministry to help prepare you? Why is this needed?
5. What "next steps" make sense for you to take in pursuing vocational ministry?

Epilogue

For Those Who Don't Desire Vocational Ministry

Isaac was despondent. After attending a conference on the urgency and need for young adults to serve as foreign missionaries, he thought he'd have some personal word from God that would compel him to abandon his vocational dreams, go overseas, and serve. He knew the ministry leaders at his church were praying that God would raise up missionaries, and so were his parents. There was even some expectation and hope that he'd be the next great global missionary who'd inspire a whole generation to sacrifice for the cause of Christ. Except Isaac didn't feel this was what God wanted him to do.

There were no great lights from above. No glorious visions of global movement and success. Not even a low whisper or humble nudge. Isaac would admit the preaching was good. He was encouraged by the Bible teaching about God's glory. He was well informed about the problem of thousands (millions!) of people headed to a Christless eternity. He was encouraged to pray more earnestly for the equipping and sending of global missionaries. Yet he didn't feel that going was *his* task. He didn't sense any compulsion from the Lord to drop his education in business and go to seminary. As a result, he was deeply discouraged. Was he doing something wrong?

He wondered if he'd missed something. Maybe he wasn't as close to the Lord as he should've been. Perhaps he had some secret, even unknown, sin, and now the anticipated anointing and calling of God were revoked. He wondered if God held him in lesser regard because he didn't feel the calling that the speakers were advocating. Isaac was frustrated and felt like a failure. Was he being disobedient to God, or was he free not to pursue ministry?

Maybe, after reading this book, you don't feel as conflicted as Isaac. Yet you may share his frustration or confusion as you think about your ambitions for the future. You might wonder what it means if you don't desire to go into vocational Christian leadership. Specifically, you might wonder what this means for your relationship with God and your life as a Christian. Let me give you four encouragements about what's next for you if you don't feel called into full-time Christian ministry.

Not Everyone Is Called to Vocational Christian Leadership

Yes, one of the primary goals of this book is to help encourage young adults like yourself to consider careers in Christian ministry and leadership. But that doesn't mean everyone should do it. Most shouldn't. While the next 25 years are critical to determining what Christianity will look like in the West, that doesn't mean all will be lost unless you answer the call to change your career direction and go into ministry. God has given you desires, interests, abilities, and passions that make you unique. He has made a place for you to glorify him, regardless of whether it's in formal Christian leadership or not.

There's no shortage of opportunity for your life to bring tremendous glory to God in any vocation or career pursuit. Whatever field you go into, as God's child you'll be in a unique position to make him known in the use of your gifts and in service to others. Everything you do will be an opportunity to be his ambassador. Paul encourages us, "Whatever you do, in word or in deed, do everything in the name of the Lord Jesus, giving thanks to God the Father through him" (Col. 3:17, CSB).

When God's people were exiled to Babylon, he didn't tell them to become prophets or preach to the pagan Babylonians. While he did place some of them in positions where they could bear faithful witness and influence the empire's leaders, to the large population of Jewish exiles, he said,

> Build houses and live in them. Plant gardens and eat their produce. Find wives for yourselves, and

> have sons and daughters. Find wives for your sons and give your daughters to men in marriage so that they may bear sons and daughters. Multiply there; do not decrease. Pursue the well-being of the city I have deported you to. Pray to the Lord on its behalf, for when it thrives, you will thrive. (Jer. 29:5–7, CSB)

Essentially, he was calling them to live ordinary lives as distinct people of God amid a foreign and ungodly culture. If formal Christian ministry isn't in your future, don't despair. Pursue the good vocation you're preparing for right now. Grow as an adult and be a faithful follower of Christ in your life's ordinary and everyday realities. God is for you in those pursuits! Among God's people, no vocations are more blessed or approved by God than others. A pastor or missionary has no higher or more glorious standing before the Lord than an engineer or teacher. Just do what God has laid before you to do as his servant (Col. 3:23–24).

Reject an Identity in a Career

One of the prominent confusions of our era is that we are what we do. We can build our identities around our careers. For those in Christian ministry, we can believe the lie that God accepts us because we serve him 24 hours a day, 7 days a week, 365 days a year. I *must* be really important because I'm a pastor or worship leader or children's ministry director. The tragedy in making my vocation my identity is that if I ever ceased being a pastor, what would I be and how would God relate to me?

Would I be shoved down the ladder of heavenly importance if I was "just an ordinary Christian"?

Here's where we need to preach the gospel to ourselves a lot. God doesn't accept you and me based on what we've done. God doesn't love us more if we serve him in Christian ministry. We aren't less loved if we work blue-collar jobs in an automotive factory.

The gospel's good news is that God accepts, approves, adopts, and showers love and affection on us based on the work of someone else—Jesus Christ, the Son of God. It's Jesus who won righteousness for us in his perfect work of active obedience to the Father. Jesus satisfied the penalty and shame of our failures by becoming a curse and enduring the shame of the cross on our behalf. Jesus rose from the dead on the third day in triumph to give new and eternal life to those who trust him. If you've placed your faith in Jesus and all his work, then you have a distinct and enduring identity as a loved child of God, which is superior to any identity a job could provide.

Renounce any deceptive lies that tell you your status and acceptance with God are based on whether you're in "sacred" ministries instead of "secular" occupations. Jesus gives you a more excellent and glorious name than any title could provide.

"Ministry" isn't something that just happens in a church building or Christian organization setting. Wherever you are in proximity to other people, you have a space to help them know and love Jesus. A Christian business owner can be a faithful manager of his company and employees by paying them a good wage and leading them well to achieve company objectives. A middle-school teacher can love her students and help them develop academically and socially, and—as opportunity presents—offer care and spiritual direction. Paul told the Colossians who didn't work in ministry settings to "work heartily, as for the Lord and not for men, knowing that from the Lord you will receive the inheritance as your reward" (Col. 3:23–24).

Support Those Who Are Called

One of the best things you can do if you don't sense a future in full-time Christian ministry is to advocate for and support those who do. Be an active, serving, and giving member of your local church. The romantic view of Christian ministry is the one of a lone, called, and set apart individual charging the gates of hell to rescue as many as possible. The reality, however, is that no one can (or should!) venture into Christian ministry on his own. What will make a difference in the next 25 years isn't solitary "influencer" pastors shooting out hot takes from their sermons onto social media. No, the effect will be made by communities of local Christians, including those serving in vocational ministry, working together to love God, serve their neighbors, and bear faithful gospel witness in their cities and neighborhoods. For those ministries to be sustained and flourish, it'll take the combined prayers, finances, and time of all God's people.

One of the best things you can do as a follower of Jesus is to be ordinary. Pursue a great career in something that inspires and motivates you. Find a job in that industry and get to work. Become a member of a local church and begin serving there. Give generously of your earnings to support your local church's ministry. Pray for your leaders. Host global missionaries in your home and support their labors and work. Be an ordinary member of the church. Tim Keller writes,

> Not only are the most modest jobs—like plowing a field or digging a ditch—the "masks" through which God cares for us, but so are the most basic social roles and tasks, such as voting, participating in public institutions, and being a father or mother. These are all God's callings, all ways of doing God's work in the world, and all ways through which God distributes his gifts to us.[1]

God's work of building his church and advancing his gospel is done through the ordinary contributions of life that his people invest in, and through the local church. Support those who are especially called, and the church will flourish as a community together.

Make It Your Ambition

One final encouragement I want to share with you is to embrace the first six pursuits I shared in this book. Not everyone is called to vocational Christian ministry. But every follower of Jesus should live with a compelling passion to know and love God. Each of us, whether a pastor or a plumber, should seek to emulate Christ's character in our life. All believers should know who they are in the sense of their gifts, abilities, and talents—and use those gifts for the gospel's sake. If we're called to

1. Keller and Alsdorf, *Every Good Endeavor* (Dutton, 2012), 71.

love our neighbor as ourselves (Matt. 22:39), we should make sure our vocations and day-to-day lives carry out the purpose of serving others, not just ourselves. Every Christian is an ambassador of King Jesus in this world. Therefore, we should be eager to share the gospel with the non-Christians in our spheres. Finally, each of us will face an appointed and allotted share of suffering and hardship. We should dedicate ourselves to persevering and walking through that hardship, seeking to become more like Jesus as we suffer.

You may not have any desire or compulsion to become a teacher in a Christian school, a pastor of a local church, or a staff member with a campus ministry at a university. That's OK, even commendable. However, you must have *some* ambition or trajectory in your life. Too many today are living with no ambition or vision for their lives. We've become a culture that's "entertaining ourselves to death"[2] rather than accomplishing great and noble things. We've become entitled and satisfied with luxuries and comforts that have seduced us to sleep. Instead of pursuing significant purposes and ambitions for Christ, we're piddling away our lives with trivialities. It may seem paradoxical to tell you in one paragraph "Be ordinary" then in the next to say "Aspire to something!" Yet you can live an ordinary, quiet life of faithful work and service to Christ. When Paul heard about believers in Thessalonica quitting their jobs and living aimless, idle lives, he urged them "in the name of the Lord Jesus

2. This idea plays off Neil Postman's classic work *Amusing Ourselves to Death: Public Discourse in the Age of Show Business*, 20th anniversary ed. (1985; Penguin Books, 2006).

Christ to settle down and work to earn their own living . . . [and to] never get tired of doing good" (2 Thess. 3:12–13, NLT).

At the end of almost every significant sporting event, journalists will be down on the field interviewing the athletes. Without exception, they'll talk to the star performers and ask how they won the game, what they were thinking during the contest, and what motivated them to succeed. Usually, athletes will say generic things about it being a team effort (if a team was involved) or thank their coach. They'll mention the preparation and energy that went into getting them to that moment. Then the journalists will ask, "What happened in that pivotal moment of the contest that propelled you to victory?" I love it when an athlete says, "We knew we could win this game and were the better team. We just had to go out there and *leave it all on the field*."

Friend, whatever you do in your life, I encourage you not to aim at earthly pursuits or ambitions. Don't fix your goals on the inconsequential and insignificant. Set your eyes on Jesus; set your eyes on heavenly things. Put your energy toward ultimate endeavors, kingdom-of-God-aspirations, and eternity-enduring efforts. Seek to know and love God and to make him known. Like that star athlete, at this pivotal moment in your life and the history of the world, get grand ambitions for God's glory and go *leave it all on the field*.

Acknowledgments

If any of my writing has come as a surprise to me, this book is probably the biggest. As I was writing my last book, *Pastor, Jesus Is Enough*, my children, especially Ethan, would frequently ask, "When are you going to write the children's book?" What they were really asking was when I was going to write a book specifically for them. At the time, I didn't have an answer (and I didn't imagine myself as a children's book writer). So when Jared Kennedy approached me about writing a book encouraging young adults to consider vocational ministry, I saw God's providence in opening a door to fulfill that desire to write for my children as well as for an emerging generation of young Christians.

I'm deeply grateful to Jared for his pursuit of me and invitation to work with The Gospel Coalition in producing this resource. His brainstorming, confidence, and encouragement along with his editorial hand have brought this concept to reality. Ruth Castle and Cassie Watson have improved the manuscript all the more with their helpful edits and insight, along with the rest of the TGC editorial team. I'm also encouraged by and appreciative of Trevin Wax and his willingness to carve out time to write the foreword to introduce me and these godly ambitions to our readers. His support has been invaluable.

A few friend-editors have read these chapters and offered helpful improvements and clarification. Allison Writebol has been my first reader all along and helped me keep the target audience squarely in sight as I write. Josh Carrillo and Darren Nelson provided pastoral and leader-oriented insight and wisdom throughout the manuscript. I'm so grateful for these two brothers and their hearts for Christ and the next generation. Ronnie "Kringle" Martin helped me navigate through a certain conundrum I'd created as I was wrapping up the manuscript.

A ministry of public writing is always a community experience. The congregation I serve at Woodside Bible Church Plymouth has been a tremendous source of support in prayer and encouragement. My home Life Group especially prayed with me and for me throughout the process. I'm also grateful for the affirmation and support of Pastor Chris Brooks and other leaders at Woodside as I've written. I hope this book serves our church and the young adults across our campuses, in Collective, and through The Leadership Institute for a long time.

My greatest supporter and prayer partner has been my wife, Stephanie. Without her encouragement and support in life and ministry, I wouldn't have the time or freedom to write. I'm so blessed with her as my friend and wife. She's provided ideas and insights to this project, and her prayers are fingerprints all over this work. Thank you, Steph, for loving me and being a steady source of encouragement in ministry and writing. I love you. Let's live right on!

Most of all, I'm grateful to God for his grace to rescue me from my sin, adopt me into his family, and appoint me for ministry to serve and proclaim him. May he take this work as an offering to him and use it to glorify himself and raise up this generation to glorify and enjoy him forever.

Soli Deo gloria.

General Index

Scripture Index

"Rebecca McLaughlin offers a gentle, yet powerful biblical corrective that calls readers to holistic Christian love a higher calling than the call of the culture, and, often, a harder calling. She examines popular cultural mantras and answers each one with the truth and application of the gospel of Christ. In her balanced and gracious approach, she paints our culture's arguments in the most compassionate light possible and then shows the beauty of a more excellent way!"

Jasmine Holmes, author of *Mother to Son: Letters to a Black Boy on Identity and Hope*

Also Available from the Gospel Coalition

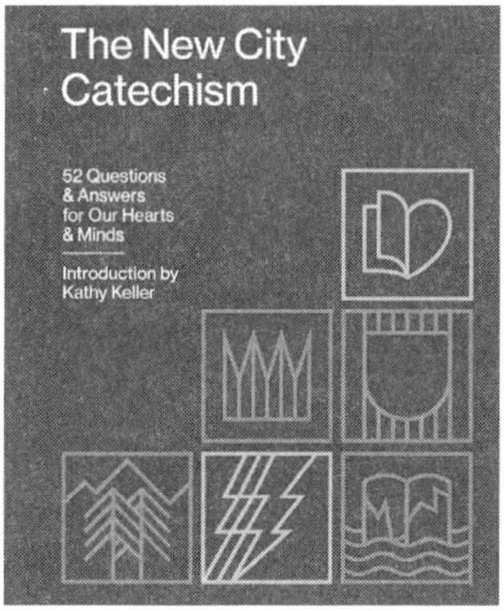

THE GOSPEL COALITION

The Gospel Coalition (TGC) supports the church in making disciples of all nations, by providing gospel-centered resources that are trusted and timely, winsome and wise.

Guided by a Council of more than 40 pastors in the Reformed tradition, TGC seeks to advance gospel-centered ministry for the next generation by producing content (including articles, podcasts, videos, courses, and books) and convening leaders (including conferences, virtual events, training, and regional chapters).

In all of this we want to help Christians around the world better grasp the gospel of Jesus Christ and apply it to all of life in the 21st century. We want to offer biblical truth in an era of great confusion. We want to offer gospel-centered hope for the searching.

Join us by visiting TGC.org so you can be equipped to love God with all your heart, soul, mind, and strength, and to love your neighbor as yourself.